Fashion for the People

A
History
of
Clothing
at
Marks & Spencer

Rachel Worth

BERG

Oxford • New York

English edition
First published in 2007 by
Berg
Editorial offices:
First Floor, Angel Court, 81 St Clements Street, Oxford OX4 1AW, UK
175 Fifth Avenue, New York, NY 10010, USA

Berg is the imprint of Oxford International Publishers Ltd.

This book has been produced with the support of the Arts and
Humanities Research Council

Arts & Humanities
Research Council

Library of Congress Cataloging-in-Publication Data
Worth, Rachel.
  Fashion for the people : a history of clothing at Marks & Spencer /
Rachel Worth. — English ed.
    p. cm.
  Includes bibliographical references and index.
  ISBN-13: 978-1-84520-173-9 (cloth)
  ISBN-10: 1-84520-173-6 (cloth)
  ISBN-13: 978-1-84520-174-6 (pbk.)
  ISBN-10: 1-84520-174-4 (pbk.)
  1. Clothing trade—Great Britain—History. 2. Marks & Spencer
plc—History. I. Title.

  TT496.G7W67 2007
  391.0941'0904—dc22   2006027932

British Library Cataloguing-in-Publication Data
A catalogue record for this book is available from the British Library.

    ISBN-13   978 1 84520 173 9 (Cloth)
              978 1 84520 174 6 (Paper)
    ISBN-10   1 84520 173 6 (Cloth)
              1 84520 174 4 (Paper)

Typeset by Avocet Typeset, Chilton, Aylesbury, Bucks
Printed and bound by CPI Group (UK) Ltd, Croydon, CR0 4YY

www.bergpublishers.com

Fashion

for

the

People

To my son, Samuel

CONTENTS

LIST OF FIGURES

All photos appear courtesy of the Marks & Spencer Archive.

ACKNOWLEDGEMENTS

I would like to thank the following people for their involvement and generously given support in the preparation of this book: Rebecca Arnold, Alison Cork, Paul Jobling, Philippa McMinn, Brian White and Emma Worth. I am grateful to the Arts and Humanities Research Council (AHRC) and the Arts Institute at Bournemouth for supporting this project by granting me study leave in 2005 in order for this project to be brought to fruition.

The text draws on a broad range of unpublished material in the Marks & Spencer Archive, and I am sincerely grateful to Lord Stone (formerly Marks & Spencer joint managing director) for supporting this project from the early 1990s and for initially giving me access to the wealth of information afforded by this invaluable resource. I would also like to thank Susan Breakell (former Marks & Spencer archivist) and Rebecca Walker (Marks & Spencer archivist) for their unstinting time in helping me to navigate my way around the archive, and Heather MacRae for arranging permission to publish illustrations courtesy of the Marks & Spencer Archive.

A large number of Marks & Spencer personnel also provided me with many fascinating insights and a range of perspectives. The majority of these people have since departed the company. Those whom I interviewed formally are acknowledged in the notes of relevant chapters and their job title at the time of interview is given. Many others offered me the benefit of their thoughts and experiences on a number of different occasions. In particular, I must thank Sheilagh Brown, Martin Clarkson, Ismar Glasman, Brian Godbold, Lewis Goodman, Richard Lachlan, Alan Lambert, Jane Harrison (Miller), Clinton Silver, and Sara Stephenson (Gottgens). Thanks also to Michael Terry of Dewhirst.

THE MARKS & SPENCER ARCHIVE

The existence of the archive owes much to the foresight and interest of Marks & Spencer's first archivist, the late Paul Bookbinder. Established in 1984 in order to conserve the company's collection of historic documents and artefacts, the archive is in the process of being catalogued. Researched over the course of nearly a decade, the documents selected as reference and for discussion in this study are listed in the Bibliography and include the following: unpublished histories of the company, memos and correspondence written by Marks & Spencer personnel, papers relating to technological initiatives, design briefs, records of stocks and sales (checking lists), chairman's statements, company publications including *St Michael News*, *M&S World* and back copies of *The M&S Magazine*. The range of visual and photographic material (store frontages and window displays) is evidenced by the illustrations selected. The archive also holds a substantial collection (over 1,500 articles) of surviving dress. Keren Protheroe (2005) gives a useful overview of the scope of the archive.

The in-house publication, *St Michael News*, provides the most comprehensive coverage of the range and extent of the clothing ranges, from the 1950s, and gives invaluable insights into corporate perceptions. In order to mark a new phase in the company's history after the demise of the Utility clothing scheme, the first issue of *St Michael News* (distributed free to all members of staff) appeared in June 1953. From August 1955 it went into regular fortnightly publication. Its aim was to inform staff members of the latest company news, including product information, store openings and extensions, long-service celebrations, work done for charity in the community, the company's latest financial figures, and information on key Marks & Spencer personnel. So far as this study is concerned, the most significant aspect of *St Michael News* is its extensive coverage of the clothing Marks & Spencer sold, along with the latest fashion news (from a corporate perspective, of course) and detailed discussion of technological innovations affecting the manufacture of new, easy-care fabrics (especially from the 1950s). From the late 1980s, this information is supplemented by that provided by *The M&S Magazine*, the first edition of which was published in time for Christmas 1987. References to individual numbers of *St Michael News*, *The M&S Magazine* and *M&S World* are cited in the text and listed in the Bibliography.

Rachel Worth

There are elaborate and instructive histories of costume, but they are dedicated to the richer classes. Nobody has thought it expedient or even interesting to record the evolution of the clothing of the broad masses of the nation.

Harry Sacher, unpublished history[1]

The 'new' dress history, whilst redressing the weight of research away from endless publications on couture clothing, has still failed to assess in any serious depth issues surrounding the design, manufacture, retailing and consumption of urban working-class dress in Western cultures in the nineteenth and twentieth centuries.

Lou Taylor, *The Study of Dress History*

Marks & Spencer (the focus of this study), along with the company's principal competitors, F. W. Woolworth (founded 1909), Littlewoods (founded 1923) and British Home Stores (founded 1928), expanded rapidly in the first half of the twentieth century, and by 1939 these chains together had around 1,200 stores in Britain, and commanded nearly 20 per cent of the total sales achieved by multiple retail organizations (Jeffreys 1954: 69–70). Writing from the perspective of the 1950s, Margaret Wray's account (1957) is enlightening. She observes that Marks & Spencer was 'the earliest variety chain store group to undertake the distribution of women's outerwear' and that 'they are still the most important and progressive group in this field' (Wray 1957: 36). Indeed, by the mid-1980s, the influence of Marks & Spencer was such that it was claimed that the single most important reason for the regional shopping centre boom of that period was the decision by the company to enter the Metro Centre in Gateshead (Guy 1994: 174). Those studies that concentrate on the retail development process fully acknowledge the significance of the history of the development of the multiple chain store (originally known as the variety chain store). However, the latter's contribution, since the 1920s, to the *clothing* of millions of people – both in the UK and, as retailers expanded their empires, in the rest of Europe and beyond – has not been credited with the importance it deserves. In spite of the fact that, as Susannah Frankel estimated for the late 1990s, there were fewer than 2,000 customers worldwide who bought the most expensive made-to-measure outfits (*The Guardian*, 7 February 1998: 38), the primary focus of the dress historian and the fashion commentator has been on the top end of the fashion business and on the significance of high-profile fashion designers. In contrast, in Britain, by the 1990s Marks & Spencer had the largest market share of any single retailer for clothing as a whole: 14.1 per cent in 1993, 14.5 per cent in 1994 and 14.7 per cent in 1995 (*Verdict on Clothing Retailers*, 1996: 20). For the same dates, the Burton Group (including Debenhams) came second with 10.1, 9.7 and 9.3 per cent respectively (ibid.).

So why has the emphasis in the history of dress been on fashionable and elite clothing, with its focus on spectacle and fantasy, and why has the study of 'ordinary' and 'real' clothing been neglected? These questions provide a context and starting point for this study. Jennifer Craik observes that 'while some parts of the everyday fashion system are directly attuned to elite fashion codes, most aspects have an indirect, oppositional or remote relationship with elite fashion' (Craik 1993: xi). It is therefore difficult to account for the concentration on 'high fashion' and there are indeed, as Craik observes, 'competing and contradictory fashion histories waiting to be written' (ibid.: x). It is hoped that this book will constitute just one of many such studies.

This seemingly ingrained prejudice both within the fashion industry and in fashion and dress studies may be explained, at least in part, by the disproportionate influence couture exerts on the dissemination of new fashion trends, and the ability of individual fashion designers to exercise their influence and talent on our aesthetic aspirations. The assumption is that retailers and consumers will follow the styles set by high fashion. Although far from providing an adequate way of explaining the dynamics of changes in fashion, the 'trickle-down theory'[2] has tended to shift attention away from an interest in ordinary fashion. Significantly, Leopold (1992) argues that it is the (false) division made between the history of production and that of consumption which has resulted in 'a tendency to view the history of fashion from the top down, rather than the bottom up – as the history of haute couture, in other words' (Leopold 1992: 102). The history of fashion has overlooked the slow but sustained development of mass markets for cheap standardized clothing and 'concentrated instead on the differentiation and diffusion of production emanating from a much narrower segment of the market which, despite its limited scope, has nonetheless attracted a disproportionate share of media attention' (ibid.).

Lou Taylor points out that by far the greatest emphasis in fashion publications and exhibitions is still on the most glamorous levels of clothing production – garments of the top 0.5 per cent of the wealthy of Europe and the USA (Taylor 2002: 51). Furthermore, and notwithstanding the fact that 'mass-produced clothing has for over 150 years been a major national industry and one that has had massive political, social and cultural ramifications … there have been no major national exhibitions in Britain which have examined in any depth ready-to-wear clothing design, manufacture and style diffusion, let alone consumption' (ibid.). Although the 1994–5 *Street*

Style exhibition at the V&A Museum, London, refreshingly chose an alternative to couture and high fashion as its subject, by focusing on specific 'street' styles (for example 'zooties', 'bikers' and 'skinheads'), it placed itself outside the perspective of what can be described as an exhibition of 'ordinary clothing'.[3] But it is precisely the 'ordinariness' of Marks & Spencer and high-street fashion that seems to have excluded their inclusion in such studies.

Published literature discussing the clothing sold by high-street retailers constitutes a minority of the total body of work relating to fashion studies.[4] Elizabeth Wilson and Lou Taylor's 1989 study, *Through the Looking Glass: A History of Dress from 1860 to the Present Day* (which accompanied the BBC television series), unusually and insightfully considers the changing social context that made ready-made clothing acceptable and even desirable to women. Other histories of twentieth-century fashion, such as Elizabeth Ewing's *History of 20th Century Fashion* (1993 [1974]), also place developments in fashion within their social context and in relation to economic and technical change, and discuss the role of retailers with references to Marks & Spencer. However, the whole texts devoted specifically to Marks & Spencer, though very useful in providing accounts of the history of the company, do not discuss in detail the significance of the company's contribution from the perspective of fashion history.[5]

This book will suggest ways in which social and cultural history – arguably the most obvious umbrella discipline to provide a framework for a discussion of the clothing of 'the broad masses of the nation' (Sacher, unpublished history, V: 30) – can provide a useful starting point for the key issues addressed by this study. The decision on the part of Marks & Spencer to sell clothing, from the mid-1920s, and the sheer range of products retailed by the company only a decade later – in particular women's clothing – reveals how retailers were able to respond to, and stimulate, for example, technological developments within the ready-to-wear clothing industry. That decision also bears witness to shifts in class structures and social roles, both cause and effect of changes in lifestyles commanded by women not normally considered to be in a position, financially at least, to aspire to being 'fashionable'. From the 1930s onward, further technological and design developments affecting the quality and the look of mass-produced clothing, coupled with changes in the retail environment and the 'shopping experience', as well as new ways in which clothing retailers communicated to their customers about the products being sold, created the phenomenon of 'high-street clothing' as we understand it today. In short, a highly diverse and complex system of the mass retailing of clothing on the high street has become an integral and commonplace part of everyday living and one which is so familiar that at the start of the twenty-first century, it is difficult to imagine a time when it did not exist. This cultural transformation is an aspect of history that has hitherto been neglected, and to this extent the history of clothing and the way in which clothing has been marketed and sold via the retailer must surely constitute a significant part of social and cultural history. The words of the cultural historian Daniel Roche (albeit articulated in a different context) are relevant here: 'A new problematic of the history of clothing is a way of penetrating to the heart of social history' (Roche 1994: 5). Not only can an assessment of Marks & Spencer's contribution enrich both social and cultural history, but it can also inform a dialogue in respect of the influence of mass fashion retailing on wider consumer culture.

However, until relatively recently, disciplines other than those which have directly concerned themselves with the study of dress – such as economic and social history – have, in the main, failed to address the study of clothing as indicative of, and impinging upon, cultural and social milieus in other than broadly empirical terms. Given the way in which English social history was first conceived as the 'history of the people' (Wilson 1993: 10) and social history's self-image as 'the new history' in opposition to 'traditional history' (ibid.: 21), it is perhaps ironic that the history of dress and, in particular, the history of dress of 'the people', has not yet found a truly comfortable place within social history. The social historian Margaret Spufford, whose work is an exception in this context, neatly summarized the situation as she saw it in the 1980s, noting that 'the social historian does not normally look at histories of costume with a serious analytical eye' and 'the sources used by historians of costume have been almost entirely noble and gentle ones' (Spufford 1984: 98–9). One of the principal objectives of this study, therefore, is to consider ways in which the history of non-elite clothing, as exemplified by the ranges retailed by Marks & Spencer, can and should make a significant contribution to social and cultural history and hence how fashion and dress may be studied in the context of this perspective. In this respect much has already been achieved over the past three decades, not only in terms of forging links between the history of dress and other academic disciplines, but by challenging the methodological framework and parameters of a traditional, largely object-based dress history.

A seismic shift occurred within dress history circles in the 1990s, in so far as the subject became more overtly self-critical and opened its doors to contributions from across academic divides. The Costume Society's annual conference of 1997 (held in Manchester and celebrating the fiftieth anniversary of the Gallery of English Costume at Platt Hall), entitled 'Dress in History: Studies and Approaches', both reflected and provided a further stimulus to this process. It encouraged debate about where the study of dress 'fits', with potential bids made by academics adopting approaches derived from, for example, art history, design history, and social and cultural history. 'Dress history', John Styles observed in 1998, 'is now a point of intersection for scholars coming from a wide variety of disciplinary backgrounds' (Styles 1998: 388). Styles exhorted historians of dress to 'recognize and embrace the conceptual diversity of current historical scholarship', arguing that 'acknowledgement of this diversity is the key to putting the study of dress back into history' (ibid.). In addition, the publication *Fashion Theory*, its subtitle significantly framed as *The*

Journal of Dress, Body and Culture (first published in 1997) also evidenced this spirit of collaboration, open-mindedness and inclusiveness, bringing together writings whose principal focus was a study of dress and the body, written from a large range of different academic perspectives: cultural studies, anthropology and ethnography, to name but a few. In essence, the positive result has been, on the one hand, a recognition of the significance of dress by academic disciplines which previously accorded it little or no attention and, on the other, consideration by dress historians (those academics principally concerned with the study of *dress* rather than with the utilization of dress to elicit further analysis of their own discipline) of approaches and methodologies which would further develop the study of the subject. These developments have been both chronicled and progressed substantially by seminal texts such as *The Culture of Fashion: A New History of Fashionable Dress* by Christopher Breward (1995), *Defining Dress: Dress as Object, Meaning and Identity* by Amy de la Haye and Elizabeth Wilson (eds.) (1999) and, more recently, *The Study of Dress History* by Lou Taylor (2002). No academic discipline stands still, and it is hoped that in the future dress history will become more clearly defined by its own discrete methodological framework. It is hoped that this study will contribute to that process.

The focus of this book is the contribution made by Marks & Spencer to the *democratization* of fashion. Rather than attempt to define 'democratization' too narrowly at this stage, or to use it solely to categorize a movement towards 'mass fashion' or 'mass production' during the inter-war period, discussion within individual chapters will help to delimit the boundaries of a possible definition or definitions. In general terms, however, the term is taken here to mean the process by which fashion and style, rather than being primarily the preserve of the rich, become increasingly accessible to a much broader range of people than hitherto, in a diverse range of social and economic circumstances. In the context of this study, democratization does not just mean that the provision of clothing by Marks & Spencer and other retailers simply enabled a greater section of the population to 'emulate' the styles and quality of clothing consumed by the middle and upper classes (although in certain cases it did). This book argues that the provision of clothing by the chain-store multiples actually altered definitions of fashion through the creation of *high-street fashion*. Using Marks & Spencer as a case study, it analyses the ways in which the pioneering of technical processes at all stages of production and the mass retailing and marketing of clothing have dramatically altered the consumer's perceptions of fashion. For example, the ranges of Terylene skirts sold by Marks & Spencer (Fig. 1) and other retailers in the 1950s were successful not only because of their price but because they could be drip-dried and required little or no ironing. The qualities of these garments tapped into a need in the market for good-quality, reasonably priced and easy-care clothing, the provision of which then tended to increase demand. This process reveals the complexity of changes in fashion and, in particular, the interplay between the production and the supply of clothing in relation to demand and the consumer.

1: Window display of St Michael Terylene skirts, Swansea store, 1957.

Kidwell and Christman (1974) addressed the democratization of dress in a publication accompanying an exhibition on the subject at the National Museum of History and Technology, Washington, DC. Interestingly, the perspective here is on both the production of garments and their consumption. The authors refer to a 'double revolution' in the making and wearing of clothing (Kidwell and Christman 1974: 7) and they recognize that changes in production processes affecting the look and the quality of clothing need to be considered alongside the market in which they are to be worn. In other words, the authors recognize that technological innovation cannot take place in a vacuum and without a knowledge that the goods produced will then be purchased, albeit with the help of skilful marketing. Alongside mass production was the successful mass retailing of clothing: in the USA, 'even before the mid-nineteenth century the retailing of ready-made clothing was in high gear' (ibid.: 17). Not only did ready-made clothing take off in the USA due to sophisticated production techniques, but it appeared to suffer less from a reputation for poor quality than in the UK (see Chapter 1). The authors argue that the 'disreputable' sector of the ready-to-wear industry – the production of 'slops' for the poor – 'has little to do with the democracy of dress'. Ready-to-wear clothing was more likely to be acceptable to a society where the hierarchies of clothing were less obviously dictated by the tradition of complex class structures than they were in the UK: 'ready-made clothing begat the democratization of clothing and parallels its progress' (ibid.: 15).

The issue of the democratization of fashionable dress has also been considered, albeit from a different perspective (specifically that of London) by Christopher Breward, Edwina Ehrman and Caroline Evans in *The London Look: Fashion from Street to Catwalk* (2004) and the accompanying exhibition. Both this and work such as Frank Mort's analysis of the retailing of the mass-produced suit and his work on the Burton's menswear multiple (1996 and 1997) suggest ways in which the high street is beginning to be considered seriously as a site of fashion culture. As Breward (2003: 143) states:

> The shop in its broadest definition is the last significant staging post in the trail of the product from design and manufacture to the intimate realm of the wearer, and as such the strategies by which its goods are presented for sale are of prime importance in establishing a sense of what fashion is at any given time or place.

Breward's observation is entirely relevant in relation to Marks & Spencer.

A study of Marks & Spencer and the retailing and marketing of clothing is contingent also on issues surrounding debates on consumption. As de la Haye points out, 'In recent years, consumption studies have given dress due recognition, explicitly using it as one of the most reliable indexes charting the growth of consumer society' (de la Haye and Wilson 1999: 5–6). Mica Nava et al.'s study (1997) argues that 'consumption is a new meeting place, a point of intersection which facilitates encounters between disciplines' (Nava et al. 1997: 1–2). Although history as a generic discipline has not in the past given academic weight to the importance of the history of fashion, it is partly the recognition of the significance of *consumption* as an analytical concept that has drawn historians to consider dress as relevant to their own field of interest.

For the discipline of history per se, McKendrick, Brewer and Plumb's 1982 study represented a milestone, addressing as it did head-on 'the key questions of the roots and rise of consumer capitalism' (Brewer and Porter 1993: 1). It may be seen as a reaction against the orthodoxy in economic history with its emphasis on supply/production-type explanations and serves as a critique of historians who have been 'far more interested in explaining how and why supply increased than in explaining how and why the products of that rising tide of industrial production were absorbed by the market' (McKendrick, Brewer and Plumb 1982: 97). The work of Neil McKendrick – who argued that as early as the eighteenth century, fashion filtered down to all classes (ibid.: 40) – is of particular relevance here. In spite of the criticism subsequently levelled at McKendrick's work, not only from the perspective of a consumption studies approach, but also from that of dress history,[6] it is significant that McKendrick considered dress to be 'the most public manifestation of the blurring of class divisions which was so commented on' in the eighteenth century (ibid.: 53). Clothing, therefore, although not the principal focus of the study, became the backbone on which the thesis was structured, McKendrick thus highlighting its vital role in history. By implication, he also questioned assumptions about a simplistic correlation between 'poverty and unfashionable clothing' and the converse – 'wealth and access to fashionable clothing'. Likewise, this study reveals that the dynamics of fashion production and consumption do not conform easily to such an equation.

One of the perhaps inevitable consequences of the proliferation of 'consumption studies', and of the take-up by different disciplines of the concept as a tool for analysis, has been the difficulty of reaching a consensus with regard to the term itself. As Mort explains, 'Consumption has been the subject of multiple interpretations and frequently its meanings have been disputed' (Mort 1997: 15). Rather than generalizing about the term to the extent that 'consumption is evoked as a meta-concept, used to explain the most disparate historical phenomena' (ibid.), Mort advocates that the concept be broken down into its differentiated parts. Thus consumption practices need to be treated as distinct, distinguishing between production, distribution, marketing and so on. This approach explains in part the chapter structure of this study (see below).

In the approach adopted by Ben Fine and Ellen Leopold (1993), the fashion system is considered to be a 'dual' system of provision, in so far as it may be loosely defined as the 'interrelationship between highly fragmented forms of production and equally diverse and often volatile patterns of demand'. Fashion is a hybrid subject, since it is both a 'cultural phenomenon' and 'an aspect of manufacturing with the accent on production technology' (Fine and Leopold 1993: 93). It is this dual aspect of the fashion system which, Fine and Leopold argue, accounts for the fact that it has been 'a difficult subject to accommodate within a tradition of economic history in which the histories of consumption and production plough largely separate and parallel furrows' (ibid. and Leopold 1992: 101). But in the context of this study, this definition is entirely relevant. An assessment of the contribution of Marks & Spencer to the democratization of fashion necessitates not just a consideration of social context and a discussion of clothing, style and the shopping environment as 'cultural phenomena', but it also involves an analysis of production in its broadest sense: the design, manufacture and distribution/retailing of clothing.[7] Above all, none of these different elements can be treated in isolation: supply and demand are respondent to, and dependent upon, each other. If the division between the histories of production and consumption have resulted in a 'top downwards' perspective on the history of dress with little acknowledgement of the history of ordinary fashion, reconciliation of the two can result in a more balanced and less blinkered view.

Clearly, there is no established methodological approach to be adopted from a single existing academic framework. What are the implications for this study and how are we to take on board the diverse issues discussed here and incorporate them within the parameters of this book? The most fruitful approach to the study of the retailing of mass/popular fashion is one that adopts an interdisciplinary perspective. Specifically, an assessment of the contribution of Marks & Spencer to the democratization of fashion must make reference to a range of disciplines: social, economic and cultural history, business history, consumption studies and, not least, the history of dress. An analysis of the clothing retailed by Marks & Spencer necessitates an analysis of the ready-to-wear clothing industry, the design and production of merchandise and the relationship between clothing sold on the high street and 'designer' or high fashion (the traditional focus for the 'canon' of dress history). In order to attempt to bridge what Lou Taylor describes as 'the great divide' (2002: 64) between object-based and other academic approaches, a range of source material, both visual and literary/documentary is utilized.

This book argues that Marks & Spencer has influenced our shopping habits, the actual clothes we choose to wear, and the quality and performance we expect from them, even if we have never bought an item of clothing from one of the stores. In the past, the company self-consciously aimed to break down market segmentation and fragmentation in order to be accessible to the majority. Interestingly, however, what it saw as its defining strength in terms of its market identity in the 1930s, 1940s and 1950s may, more recently and in the context of an age of niche marketing, provide a clue to its corporate weakness.

It is something of a challenge for a historian to resist examining the past of Marks & Spencer in the light of the company's present fortunes, but this book does not attempt to offer an explanation of the difficulties faced by the company at the close of the twentieth century, other than in so far as the latter draw attention towards changes in, and the evolution of, the consumer market in general (see Conclusion and Postscript). However, a discussion of the contemporary market position of Marks & Spencer does reveal the extent to which the media appraisal of Marks & Spencer has to be seen in its historical perspective. In the mid-1990s, and before the company's much discussed downturn in profits at the end of the twentieth century, there was great press speculation regarding Marks & Spencer's apparent 'reinvention' of its image from dowdy and boring to fashion-conscious and exciting (see Chapters 3 and 4). Such an interpretation betrays both a misunderstanding of the nature of fashion and a lack of historical perspective and, significantly, the divergent concerns of the fashion historian and the fashion commentator. What was described as 'new' at Marks & Spencer in the 1990s had in fact already been happening to some extent in the 1950s and 1960s.

While seeking to assess the historical contribution made by the company to fashion in the twentieth century by adopting a 'case study' approach, the book also places the developments at Marks & Spencer in a broader, comparative context. The

120-year period covered by this study begins in the 1880s, when Michael Marks set up his stall at the open market in Leeds, and ends with the company's announcement of a sustained (albeit short-lived, as it turned out) programme of international expansion in 1998, soon to be followed by what some studies, such as that by Judi Bevan (2002 [2001]), have termed the company's 'fall' at the close of the twentieth century. The sequence of the chapters follows a broadly chronological narrative, although each chapter necessarily reads according to the logic of the history it describes and therefore individual chapters also have their own discrete chronology.

The early development of Marks & Spencer from the late nineteenth century is chronicled in Chapter 1 in the context of the history of the ready-to-wear clothing industry. This discussion attempts to account for the increasing interest the founder's son, Simon Marks, and his friend and business partner Israel Sieff, took in the retailing of clothing as a reflection of the growing demand for affordable garments in the context of the changing social roles of people of the working class and lower middle class. Whereas Burton's, for example, concentrated primarily on menswear, Marks & Spencer targeted women. In Chapter 2, the role of technological innovation is explored: via, for example, the establishment by Marks & Spencer of a textile laboratory in 1935, sizing and colour standardization, and the marketing of new fabrics both in-house and through the manufacturing base in the pursuit of quality, 'fashion' and own-brand (St Michael) products. Then, in Chapter 3, the extent to which Marks & Spencer's in-house design department (established in 1936), the company's relationship with suppliers' design teams and key centres of fashion, and the employment (from the 1950s) by Marks & Spencer of design consultants, contributed to the democratization of fashionable clothing increasingly further down the social scale, is discussed. An analysis of the company's formulation of advertising and promotional strategies follows in Chapter 4 via the development of the retail environment, in-house publications such as *St Michael News*, media advertising and the employment of high-profile models from the 1960s. Chapter 5 charts Marks & Spencer's increasingly significant position from the mid-1970s, not only as a household name in Britain, but also as an international player in the world of clothing retailing.

I. MARKS & SPENCER, RETAILING AND THE READY-TO-WEAR CLOTHING INDUSTRY

The extension of retailing in the nineteenth and twentieth century is a central theme in British social and economic history – a theme just as relevant to the development of modern society as the industrial revolution which preceded it.
A. Briggs, *Friends of the People: The Centenary History of Lewis's*

Fashion that used to be the privilege of the upper class is now enjoyed by almost everyone at every social level due to the democratization of fashion that was helped by mass production during the Industrial Revolution.
Y. Kawamura, *Fashion-ology: An Introduction to Fashion Studies*

The founders of Marks & Spencer – Michael Marks and his business partner Tom Spencer, and Michael's son Simon, together with Simon's lifelong friend, Israel Sieff – made a significant contribution to developments in retailing and the textile and ready-to-wear clothing industries in Britain. In the long term, these have impacted both on contemporary patterns of shopping and the consumption of clothing. This chapter chronicles the early development of the company in the context of changing retail practices and the demand for, and production of, cheap, ready-to-wear clothing.

THE EARLY YEARS: FROM MARKET STALL TO PUBLIC COMPANY, 1884–1926

Prior to Marks & Spencer's downturn in profits towards the end of the 1990s, much discussed in the national press and chronicled in some detail by Judi Bevan (2002), the story of the transformation of Marks & Spencer from its humble origins in 1884 as a stall at the open market in Leeds, to the company's enviable position in the 1990s as 'Europe's most profitable retailer' with a group turnover of over £8.24 billion in the financial year ending April 1998 (*Marks & Spencer Annual Report and Financial Statements 1998*), and pre-tax profits (to March 1998) of £1.2 billion (Bevan 2002: 3) had, not surprisingly, become the stuff of retailing legend. As Bevan observes:

> Thirteen million shoppers a week were pouring through the doors of Marks & Spencer's 286 British stores. More important, those customers were pouring out again laden with bright green, shiny plastic bags bulging with Marks & Spencer clothes, food and homeware. That May (1998), one of the sunniest and driest on record, directors and store managers alike were bedazzled by the figures.

> Business had rarely been better for Britain's largest and most trusted retailer.
> (Bevan 2002: 1)

Indeed, the success of Marks & Spencer would probably have exceeded the ambitions and most optimistic expectations of the company's founder, Michael Marks (1863–1907)[1] and those of his son, 'retail revolutionary' Simon Marks (1888–1964).[2] The history of the early development of Marks & Spencer has been well documented by Goronwy Rees (1973 [1969]: 2–30).[3] Rees describes how Michael Marks emigrated from the village of Bialystok (then Russian Poland) probably not later than 1882, fleeing persecution of the Jews in one of a series of pogroms. Like many Jewish immigrants, it is likely that Michael Marks went first to London, but he did not settle there and by 1884 he was in Leeds.

At this time, Leeds was a rapidly growing city with a population of 310,000. Owing much to the development of the canal network and then the railways, by the middle of the nineteenth century Leeds was an important communications centre for the West Riding of Yorkshire. It was a hub of the mining, manufacturing and, significantly, the clothing industries. In Leeds, Michael found a strong Jewish community of some 6,000–7,000 people concentrated mainly in the area known as the Leylands and mostly employed in the rapidly developing clothing trade (Rees 1973: 4). The story goes that Michael, looking for work, approached a man in Kirkgate and mentioned Barran's, the name of the legendary Leeds clothier (see below), and significantly one of the few words he knew in English. The man he happened to address was Isaac Dewhirst of I. J. Dewhirst Ltd at 32, Kirkgate (wholesale merchants who then sold to pedlars), who agreed to help Michael by lending him £5.[4] Michael asked if he might use the money to buy goods from Dewhirst's warehouse with the aim of then trading these in the countryside. Dewhirst agreed and thus became the company's first supplier.

When he married Hannah Cohen in 1886, Michael Marks is described as a 'licensed hawker' on his marriage certificate, even though he had by this time given up peddling. The role of the itinerant salesman had been vitally important in the distribution of goods for centuries, and there had been pedlars since at least the fourteenth century (Davis 1966: 237–47). By the nineteenth century there were also itinerant salesman known as 'Manchester Men', some of whom were substantial merchants who set out from the mills and factories with valuable stock carried by several dozen horses. In addition, 'Scotch Drapers' appeared on the retailing scene at about the same time, specializing in selling cheap textiles manufactured by the mills. They travelled on foot, but, unusually, sold on credit (unlike the ordinary hawker) and concentrated on a well-defined area so that they could call on customers every week for instalments of the money owed to them. Scotch Drapers clearly had an important role in developing new markets among the working classes.

Although it is uncertain exactly where Michael Marks began peddling, Asa Briggs believes that it was probably in the north-east, around the area of Stockton-on-Tees, and not in the West Riding of Yorkshire (Briggs 1984: 17). Michael Marks's stock was of relatively modest value compared with that of the Manchester Men and Scotch Drapers, and was probably worth no more than £20.[5] His role – like that of other travelling salesmen – was, nevertheless, extremely important in supplying goods to people who lived in remote villages and who visited the nearest town infrequently, at most on market day or for the annual fair. In spite of the expansion of a national railway network by the last quarter of the nineteenth century, the vast majority of those living in rural areas still travelled relatively small distances, reliant as they were on walking to their destination.

The advantage of peddling, from the point of view of the salesman, was that he could demand instant payment and had the best reasons for refusing credit to his customers. The practice of offering credit operated in many of the traditional fixed shops, often to the disadvantage of the shop-owner. The goods sold by the hawker could also be varied according to customer demand, since constant travelling made it easier to replenish and diversify the stock. In addition, the itinerant salesman had no shop rent and consequently no overheads, so that for someone like Michael Marks starting up in business, there were clear economic advantages. Furthermore, hawkers were not limited to the small number of customers living within a radius of 8 km (5 miles) or so of the village shop. On the other hand, however, turnover could not be other than modest and depended on how much the hawker could carry on his back at any one time. Michael's stock consisted of goods such as buttons, mending wools, pins, needles, tapes, tablecloths, woollen socks and stockings. These goods reflected the domestic needs of people on low incomes whose clothes were largely made at home or, if they could afford it, by the village dressmaker. According to a witness before a Royal Commission (1833), travelling salesmen 'call upon the families once in three weeks and I should think that half of the population get their clothing in that way' (quoted in Briggs 1956: 29).

In spite of the important role that travelling salesmen of all kinds continued to play in the second half of the nineteenth century, their number was probably slowly declining. It is a matter of conjecture whether Michael Marks gave up peddling because of the lifestyle it necessitated, or whether he realized its limitations from an economic point of view. In any case, he was clearly ambitious and did not continue peddling for long, opening a stall at the open market on Kirkgate in Leeds. The market was held two days a week, on Tuesdays and Saturdays, and because of these restrictions Michael travelled on the other days to Castleford and Wakefield in order to expand his business. However, by the time he opened his market stall in 1884 (Fig. 2) – consisting of a trestle table of 1.8 × 1.2 m (6 × 4 ft) – the open market was already losing out against the Leeds covered market (built in 1857). Before long, Michael had opened a stall here, the obvious advantages being that it gave protection

2: Painting by Van Jones for Marks & Spencer, 1955, of Michael Marks's Penny Bazaar, 1884.

from inclement weather and, probably even more important from an economic point of view, the covered market was open for trading throughout the week.[6] Michael Marks went daily to the Dewhirst warehouse to make his purchases. Here he came into contact with Tom Spencer, the firm's cashier, with whom he went into partnership when the firm of Marks & Spencer was formed on 28 September 1894.

As a licensed hawker and then on the open and covered market stalls, Michael Marks's customers were working-class people on low incomes, averaging 15 shillings (15*s*) a week (Rees 1973: 9).[7] This sector of the market was becoming increasingly significant in terms of its collective purchasing power. In any large town, especially the manufacturing districts, the peak of activity in the covered market was Saturday night, after people had normally received their wages, when they would come to buy provisions for their Sunday dinners. Hours were usually long for the shop assistants, and the introduction of gas lighting meant that business could be extended well into the evening. On a weekday, 10.00 p.m. was the normal closing time, and this was extended until midnight on Saturdays (Davis 1966: 261). At the end of the nineteenth century, it was not uncommon for some shop assistants to be working a ninety-hour week, which sometimes included Sundays (Burns 1959: 4). The struggle for the enforcement of early closing hours for shop assistants was a long and often bitter one. When Michael Marks opened his stalls in Leeds, Castleford and Wakefield it became necessary for him to employ assistants to manage the stalls, while he managed the central purchasing and distribution of goods, travelling extensively between the three towns. He strove to improve working conditions for his assistants by, for example, erecting wooden platforms for them to stand on in the market halls so that their feet would not get cold. When he opened Penny Bazaar shops, he provided gas rings on which the girls could heat their lunches (Briggs 1984: 22). This tradition of looking after staff welfare, basic as it was at this stage – Marks believed that contented workers improved business – while not entirely altruistic in intention, was clearly enlightened in the context of the time.[8]

When Michael Marks opened his stall at the covered market, he used his well-known and much-quoted slogan, 'Don't Ask the Price, It's a Penny'.[9] Because all the goods costing a penny were displayed together, customers could select whatever they wanted without having to haggle or ask the price. On one hand, Marks was thinking about practicalities: the slogan along with the layout of the stall encouraged the customers to select the item they wanted themselves, rather than having to ask the shop assistant to show it to them, thus utilizing the principle of self-selection.[10] On another level, it would appear that Marks was also trying to understand the mindset of his customers. It was not traditionally considered 'genteel' to display price tickets, or indeed tickets which could in any way be construed as 'advertising'. In the 1833 Report of the Select Committee on Manufactures and Trade, the parliamentary committee was told (regarding price tickets): 'It is not a practice that would be resorted to by those who would seek their custom from the higher class of the community … it is much more resorted to where they seek principally customers among the lower and middling classes of people' (quoted in Davis 1966: 258). Thus, the 'Don't Ask the Price, It's a Penny' slogan obviated the need even to mention price, although of course price, for those on very modest incomes, would constitute *the* significant factor in so far as making a decision to purchase was concerned. Arguably, therefore, Marks was giving his customers the respectability they sought by employing a practice that was acceptable to middle-class customers – albeit in a different retail context.

The articles sold by Michael Marks on his market stalls were diverse, falling mostly within the categories of haberdashery (for example skeins of wool, reels of black and white cotton, bundles of elastic, corset laces, safety pins, cards of buttons, darning needles, knitting needles and mushroom darners), and fancy goods (for example brooches, combs, handkerchiefs and bracelets). In fact, the items sold could include anything that might be considered useful and which fitted into the penny (1*d*) price point. It was common economic practice for haberdashers to buy cotton and thread by the pound and then disentangle it and fold it into hanks ready to be sold. Coloured sewing silks were cut into single lengths, which the customer could draw out one at a time from a large, multi-coloured bundle. This is the kind of preparation work that Michael's wife, Hannah, would have spent the evenings doing, ready for the following day's work on the market stall. Some of the original items sold by what became known as 'Penny Bazaars' still survive, and are kept at the Marks & Spencer Archive. These items include skeins of darning wool, reels of sewing thread, buttons and ribbons. In particular, they reflect the necessity of home dressmaking aids at a time when the majority of poor people made and mended their own clothes.

In 1890–91, Michael and Hannah Marks moved to Wigan with their young son, Simon, and daughter, Rebecca. At this time, Wigan was a town of about 55,000 people and although living conditions were not good, especially for those employed in the manufacturing and mining industries, there were some advantages from the Marks's point of view. As Paul Bookbinder notes, 'Its market was the oldest and largest in Lancashire and its working-class population was of the type to which his [Michael Marks's] Penny Bazaars had the strongest appeal' (Bookbinder 1993: 22). After spending four years in Wigan, Hannah, Michael and their family (now three children) moved again, this time to Manchester in 1894 (the year in which the Marks & Spencer partnership was formed). Here, Michael's son Simon met Israel Sieff (1890–1972). They both attended Manchester Grammar School and would become lifelong friends as well as business partners.

In 1897, the company's headquarters were also moved from Wigan to Manchester. By the end of 1900, there were thirty-six branches of the Marks & Spencer Penny Bazaar chain, twenty-four in market halls and twelve in shops. The following fourteen years, up until the outbreak of the First World War, would witness rapid expansion: by 1907 there were more than sixty branches distributed throughout northern England, the Midlands, Wales and London and then during the period from 1907 until 1914, the number of branches more than doubled to a total of 140. In addition, shops were beginning to outnumber Penny Bazaars in market halls or arcades. This period also witnessed a geographical shift in the pattern of stores, with the proportion of those in London increasing. In 1914, Marks & Spencer bought up the chain of shops known as the London Penny Bazaar Company, thus gaining an important foothold in the English capital (Fig. 3). Significantly, after 1909, the company began to purchase its properties rather than renting or leasing them.

In 1903, Marks & Spencer became a limited company: the firm of Marks & Spencer Ltd was registered with a capital of 30,000 £1 shares.[11] The premature death of Michael Marks in 1907, as well as that of Tom Spencer in 1905, resulted in a period of instability for the company (1908–14), during which the control and management of the company was not firmly in family hands. Simon Marks was still too young to take on his father's business, although he finally became chairman in 1916, a position he held until his death in 1964. Israel Sieff became vice-chairman and joint managing director in 1926, also the year in which Marks & Spencer became a public company. Interestingly, in the late 1920s and 1930s, the initials 'M' and 'S' became associated more with the names 'Marks and Sieff' than 'Marks & Spencer' (Briggs 1984: 46). Each eventually married the other's sister: in 1910 Israel married Simon's sister, Rebecca Marks, and in 1915 Simon married Israel's sister, Miriam Sieff. Business ties and those of friendship thus became family ties in addition, a significant factor for the future history of the company.

3: Penny Bazaar, Holloway c.1914.

During the mid-1920s (around the time when Marks & Spencer became a public company) the emphasis on clothing became increasingly important in terms of the categories of goods sold by the company. In searching for the origins of the interest by Simon Marks and Israel Sieff in the retailing of *clothing*, there are a number of links in the early years of the company's history that can be made with different aspects of the garment industry. For example, in their respective memoirs, Israel and his son Marcus Sieff describe how, prior to the pogrom of 1882, Ephraim Sieff (their father and grandfather respectively) had set up a scrap business in Königsberg, Germany, separating wool from hemp, and linen from cotton – 'recycling, as we would call it now' (M. Sieff 1988 [1986]: 14). However, like Michael Marks, Ephraim Sieff fled persecution and came to Britain, where, just before the First World War, he took over the ownership of a scrap business in Manchester, which became known as Sieff and Beaumont. Waste or scrap from tailors' cuttings was bought, sorted and graded before being sold on, probably for use in the developing ready-to-wear clothing industry. This work would have brought the Sieffs into direct contact with the particular clothing requirements of working-class customers. After his father's death, Israel inherited the company, only relinquishing the firm in the mid-1920s when most of his time became taken up with Marks & Spencer.

To those of us who assume that the current interest in second-hand clothing and concern with recycling and clothing banks is a particularly twenty-first-century phenomenon, knowledge of a pre-existing industry adds an important historical perspective. As Madeleine Ginsburg points out, the fact that clothes and textiles appear so frequently in court cases and figure so largely in the newspaper advertisements of losses and thefts in the eighteenth and nineteenth centuries is confirmation of their value (Ginsburg 1980: 123). In the nineteenth century, the second-hand clothes trade was vitally important to the working classes for the provision of relatively cheap and respectable clothing. Indeed, before the 1870s, when ready-made clothing became more readily and cheaply available (especially for men), only a very small proportion of working-class people bought new clothes (Fraser 1981: 59). The ascendancy of new clothes over good second-hand items, for poor people, probably only took place well after the turn of the twentieth century. 'Ready-made' was synonymous with 'poor quality', and in terms of both fit and fabric it was deemed inferior. Second-hand clothing therefore constituted a vitally important commodity. Jewish immigrants had traditionally participated in second-hand clothes dealing, trading widely across England, although by the middle of the nineteenth century, their numbers appear to have declined. Like Michael Marks, Jewish immigrants were frequently from tailoring or shoemaking backgrounds in their German or East European homelands, and they often sought work in the second-hand clothes trade when they arrived in Britain. By 1700, the second-hand clothing trade was centred in London, reaching its period of greatest importance in the mid-nineteenth century, by which time it was concentrated in the Rosemary Lane and Petticoat Lane areas of the East End (Ginsburg 1980: 121–5).[12]

Those clothes that were not wanted by the poorest in society were still saleable in some form or another. By the mid-nineteenth century, most fabrics could be recycled, either into fabric for clothing or for another end-product. From the sixteenth century linen, for example, had been recycled into paper. The vast quantities of rags of wool, cotton and mixtures from both home and foreign sources were shredded and spun into the yarn for 'shoddy' cloth, the staple of the growing ready-to-wear clothing industry. From about 1818, the shoddy industry had been located mainly in Batley, Yorkshire, and developments in machinery enabled even the toughest material to be turned into shoddy or 'mungo' (ibid.: 128).

In terms of Israel's own education and training in the textile business, he described how the knowledge and experience gained while working in his father's business could be applied to the work he later did at Marks & Spencer:

> I made good use of the knowledge which I had gained in this way. When Simon was staking a great deal on the production of hard-wearing garments at

competitive prices, I was able to give him information about the qualities of materials in relation to cost. When Marks & Spencer went into textiles on a very large scale, my knowledge of raw material costs was useful in dealing directly – instead of through wholesalers – with manufacturers. (I. Sieff 1970: 43)

On the Marks side of the family, meanwhile, there was a proven interest in the textile business and clothing trades. On his marriage certificate, Michael Marks entered his father's occupation as that of a tailor. A large number of Jewish immigrants into Britain in the nineteenth century were drawn into the textile and clothing industries. This was partly because of their own family traditions of work and skill in these areas, but also because they adapted more easily and willingly than their fellow workers of British origin to the introduction of the new machinery that was such an important feature of the expanding ready-to-wear industry at this period. As a consequence, however, of a buoyant and plentiful labour supply, exploitation in these industries was rife, and working conditions often appalling. Michael Marks would surely have had some knowledge of this when he arrived in Leeds. Together with his own personal ambitions, this may well explain why, from the very beginning, he pursued a path that would give him a relatively independent status. For her part, Hannah Marks maintained a deep interest in needlework and she was, according to Israel Sieff, 'a wonderful dressmaker' (I. Sieff 1970: 58).

By 1936, the textile side of the business accounted for two-thirds of the company's total sales and by 1950, Marks & Spencer was classified by the Board of Trade as a 'clothing multiple' (Rees 1973: 71). Clearly, there were many different factors influencing the decision taken by Marks & Spencer in the 1920s to concentrate on the retailing of clothing. As discussed above, some of these influences were associated with maintaining particular family interests, and knowledge and traditional skills. However, almost certainly as significant, if not more so, was the keen commercial sense and insight which enabled the Marks and Sieff families to foresee and to shape in some measure the future of the retailing of clothing. The provision and distribution of clothing lay not in traditional practices of peddling or even market stalls, but in the sale of high-quality affordable garments through a network of chain stores to an increasingly visible and discerning economic sector of the market.

In Marks & Spencer's transition from a provider of haberdashery, household necessities and fancy goods to the retailing of clothing, from the late 1920s, there were obstacles to be overcome, not least the ingrained prejudices held by many towards ready-made garments and the relative backward state of the industry in Britain. Simon Marks's formative trip to the USA in 1924 – where the ready-to-wear clothing industry was much more advanced – helped to confirm his vision for the future of Marks & Spencer. Furthermore, social and cultural changes in the aftermath of the First World War meant that the nature of the market was evolving, and with this came the demand from women for less formal, comfortable clothes with simpler constructions. The popular styles of the 1920s, with their looser fit, would lend themselves much more readily to mass production.

MARKS & SPENCER'S EXPANSION INTO CLOTHING, 1926–1936

The company's transition from selling a wide variety of goods to clothing and clothing 'accessories' (hosiery, for example) requires explanation and needs to be considered within the context of the evolving ready-to-wear clothing industry in Britain. Although Marks & Spencer's short-lived experiment in manufacturing clothing was a failure, the company maintained a close involvement with the actual production of clothing through its relationship with its suppliers. Indeed, it was Marks & Spencer personnel who frequently set the technical standards for the quality of production as much as the suppliers themselves (see Chapter 2). But to maintain a grasp of the production side of clothing was not enough: the company also responded to, and created to some extent (via the exploitation of new technology in the ready-to-wear clothing industry), changes in consumer demand – in particular, the change from home dressmaking aids (haberdashery) to ready-made clothing. As discussed in the Introduction, this is where the subject of this study bridges what must largely be artificial divides imposed between different disciplines: broadly speaking, the study of production cannot be isolated from that of consumption.

When Marks & Spencer became a public company in 1926, the prospectus of goods sold by the company was very similar to that sold by the original Penny Bazaars, the only significant addition being gramophone records. However, by the mid-1930s, the two main departments at Marks & Spencer were textiles and foods. A significant shift in policy in favour of the sale of textiles can be fairly accurately pinpointed to the decade following Simon Marks's formative trip to the USA in 1924. Harry Sacher describes the years 1928–32 in particular in terms of a 'revolution' with regard to the shift towards textiles (Sacher, unpublished history: V, 12). It is also significant that in 1928 Simon Marks introduced, among other things, a new pricing policy.

In the transition to the sale of textiles, it is clear that the price at which goods were sold was of great significance. Prior to 1914, experiments in selling goods at a range of prices other than the penny price point had been unsuccessful. Harry Sacher records that early in 1910, sixpenny (6*d*)[13] departments were opened in four branches, but they were closed down three years later (Sacher, unpublished history: III, 23). Ultimately, however, the effect of the outbreak of the First World War was to destroy the penny price point in 1915, owing to a number of different factors, not least the impact of inflation. Following the abolition of the penny price point, separate counters were introduced and goods were displayed according to their price. When Simon Marks returned from the USA, a five-shilling (5*s*)[14] limit was established, and in 1927, the policy was formally introduced. Harry Sacher recalled that at the annual general meeting of 1928, Simon Marks formally announced that: 'Our fixed price ranges do not go beyond the price of five shillings per article' (Sacher, unpublished history: IV, 28). It is highly likely that this idea originated from the American utilization of the one-dollar maximum.

The impact of the introduction of the five-shilling limit is clearly illustrated by the fact that, by 1932, over 70 per cent of the items listed in the 1926 prospectus had disappeared from Marks & Spencer stores (Rees 1973: 82). In his memoirs, Israel Sieff recalls that it was the introduction of the five-shilling price limit that affected the future development of Marks & Spencer more than any other of Simon's new policies in this period. It meant that the company had to create a whole range of goods that would fit into, and be appropriate to, the new price limit, which lasted until the outbreak of the Second World War in 1939. The profit margin, even at the level of five shillings, was small enough to require that the volume and pace of sales remained high. As Sieff recalls:

> One of its effects [the five-shilling limit] was to make textiles, and particularly women's clothing, our most important and popular line. It drove out a vast range of goods – the 'jumble' as Simon referred to it – which did not fit the modern pattern, and brought the textiles in. (I. Sieff 1970: 144)

Sieff's perspective is interesting in that it seems to assume that the economics of pricing structure rather than the demand for the product itself was what was driving the move to clothing. But the fact that the ready-to-wear clothing industry had been pioneered in the USA cannot have escaped Simon Marks's notice and this may well have determined his decision to visit in the first place. The USA had the experience of a ready-made clothing industry dating from at least the 1830s, and it is likely that Simon took careful note of the relatively advanced state of the industry there. By the 1920s, Britain was at least a decade behind the USA ready-to-wear industry, and American sizing systems were often adopted as models by British companies (see Chapter 2).

Simon Marks also brought back other 'lessons' from his trip abroad, which would be of major importance for the company's future expansion into the field of clothing; in particular, the concept of larger stores, which would allow a more effective display of merchandise (especially of clothing) (Fig. 4) and the introduction of a system of sales and stock recording, later known as the Checking List System. Marcus Sieff recalls in his memoirs that the introduction of the Checking List System in the late 1920s more effectively controlled the stocks of goods Marks & Spencer was selling. They enabled Simon to call for fortnightly reports on what was selling and what was not. They therefore acted as an invaluable gauge of consumer demand and preference. As a result of analysis of the checking lists alongside the introduction of the five-shilling maximum, clothing, Marcus Sieff observes, took on an unprecedented importance:

4: Interior of Sheffield store, c.1932.

> Clothing became the leading section of our business, three times larger than any other, and this changed the public's image of Marks & Spencer. Our growth reflected the increase in the demand for clothes, especially women's; fewer women wanted to make their own clothes at home; they wanted variety and colour, and lighter clothing for leisure. To a lesser degree this applied for men too. (M. Sieff 1988: 60–61)

The Marks & Spencer Archive retains a number of past checking lists. For the 1930s, however, these are very rare, but one dated February 1938 relating to the store in Douglas, Isle of Man is of particular interest. What is striking about this document is the sheer variety and range of clothing sold by the company at this time. Checking lists for the following clothing departments exist as follows:

(T)* 1	Boys' Wear
(T) 2	Men's Wear
(T) 3	Wool and Cotton Underwear
	Ladies' Art. [Artificial] Silk Underwear
(T) 4	[Checking list is missing, but is probably Knitted Outerwear]
(T) 5	Overalls and Mackintoshes
	Skirts
	Dresses
	Blouses
(T) 6	Ladies' Hosiery
	Children's Socks and Boys' Hose
	Men's Hose
(T) 7	Children's Wear
(T) 8	Corsetry
(T) 9	Gloves and Millinery
(T) 0	Leather Footwear, Rubber Footwear and Slippers

*Note: 'T' stands for 'textiles'. This is the abbreviation used by Marks & Spencer.
Source: unpublished papers, Marks & Spencer Archive.

The checking lists for 1938 provide an extremely useful source of information because for each department, there is a list of individual descriptions of the garments being sold. Within each department, the variety is astonishing. For example, (T) 0, leather footwear (albeit a relatively new department which had undergone rapid expansion in the early 1930s (M. Sieff 1988: 71) (Fig. 5), includes the following: babies', children's and ladies' shoes; boys' boots; youths' shoes; men's boots and shoes; wellingtons; plimsolls; slippers. This paper-based Checking List System remained in operation for over sixty years before it was replaced by a computer-based system (EPOS) in the 1980s (see Chapter 4).

Although Simon Marks's trip to the USA may have helped to confirm his ideas about the future direction of the company, Israel Sieff maintained that Simon had formulated the basis of these principles at least two years prior to this (Bookbinder 1993: 92). Indeed, it seems highly likely that he had been formulating a strategy for some time. Not only must he have been keenly aware of the continuous development of the ready-to-wear clothing industry centred in Leeds and of the potential which he saw, from an economic/production point of view, in ready-made clothes, but he was also conscious of the need for an interdependence of the output of the industry with the demands of the market, more precisely his own future customers. While he may have believed that the clothing retailed by Marks & Spencer could, to some extent, shape his customers' tastes, he was, however, ruthless when it came to eradicating lines that were clearly unpopular. By all accounts, Simon Marks was a visionary and astute businessman: the determination of future company policy

5: Shoe-buying department, head office, c.1938.

towards the emphasis on clothing, from the late 1920s onwards, must have been a considered and calculated decision. Simon Marks and Israel Sieff recognized an untapped market for the provision of good-quality, ready-made clothes. While men of the lower middle and working classes were already being catered for to some extent in terms of affordable clothing (both ready-made and wholesale bespoke suits) by shops such as Burton's and Hepworth (see below), there was no real equivalent source of clothing for women.

Marks & Spencer's main competitor in the period immediately after the First World War was the well-known American giant, F. W. Woolworth. Frank Winfield Woolworth's 'great five-cent store' was opened in 1879; by 1905 the company was incorporated as F. W. Woolworth & Co., with 120 stores in the USA. The first 3d (threepenny) and 6d (sixpenny)[15] stores were opened in England in 1909 (Liverpool), the company undergoing swift expansion so that by the end of 1912 there were an incredible 596 stores. As Marks & Spencer was a close competitor, Simon Marks and Israel Sieff would have been aware of the prices charged by Woolworth (the idea of the upper price limit was clearly an American practice, though not one that was exclusive to Woolworth). They would also have kept a close eye on the products sold by Woolworth and it is logical to argue that there must have been some urgency on the part of Marks & Spencer to explore avenues in which its main competitor did not appear to have overt ambitions. Significantly, according to Harry Sacher, in the early 1920s Marks & Spencer engaged some former Woolworth managers (Sacher, unpublished history: IV, 13). In order to appreciate the significance of Marks & Spencer's breakthrough into the retailing of clothing, it is helpful to consider the early history of the British ready-to-wear clothing industry and the prejudices companies such as Marks & Spencer had to overcome.

THE DEVELOPMENT OF THE READY-TO-WEAR CLOTHING INDUSTRY

Beverley Lemire's work (1997) on the early ready-to-wear clothing industry reveals that the industry is older than has often been assumed. By the 1930s, the ready-made garment industry was at least one hundred years old. Ellen Leopold points out the need to distinguish between the development of ready-to-wear clothing in general and factory-made clothing, arguing that in a limited sense, mass markets preceded mass production (Leopold 1992: 103). However, by the early twentieth century, it was still riddled with problems, both on the production side of the business as well as from the consumers' perspective. On one hand, the technical application of machinery to the clothing industry as a whole was uneven. The textile industry, in contrast to the apparel industry, showed all the classic features of mass production: it was heavily capitalized, highly concentrated, and was operated in large-scale production units (ibid.: 113). The clothing industry, on the other hand, was labour-intensive[16] and, as Leopold observes, continued to rely on the individually operated sewing machine well into the twentieth century (ibid.: 104). Furthermore, the industrial manufacture of women's clothing was a long way behind that of men's clothing, even at the close of the First World War.

The ingrained prejudice associated with ready-made, 'off-the-peg' clothing was not insignificant. Part of the reason for this seems to be that the styles of the nineteenth century depended on a good fit, and respectability and gentility were thus conferred via made-to-measure clothing that fitted to perfection. The ability to afford a dressmaker or, for the minority, the services of a couturier, helped to confirm class and status. For the upper classes and aspiring middle classes, the only really acceptable ready-made clothing in the late nineteenth century would have been accessories such as stockings or perhaps a shawl or mantle from a department store. This helps to explain why the sectors of the women's ready-to-wear garment industry that developed most quickly were in areas where fit was relatively unimportant, where the garment was, by its nature, loose-fitting (as in a mantle), or where the garment could be sold partly made up (as in a skirt or bodice) and could thus be altered according to the specific measurements of its wearer.

The complex construction of women's fashions in the late nineteenth century therefore helps to explain the relatively slow development of the ready-to-wear clothing industry. It follows that the looser-fitting clothes fashionable from the1920s lent themselves more easily to mass production. The importance of adequate sizing was clearly recognized by companies such as Marks & Spencer, even if, in practice, finding such a system was not always easy to achieve. The successive size surveys conducted by Marks & Spencer to improve the fit of their clothing ranges over the years (see Chapter 2) were partly responsible for breaking down prejudices associated with ready-made clothing. It is useful at this juncture to describe briefly the history of the ready-to-wear clothing industry.

In the eighteenth century, ready-made clothes could be purchased from special 'show shops'. Sailors in particular demanded clothing that could be worn immediately and was of simple construction, often referred to as 'slops' (Kidwell and Christman 1974: 27). By the beginning of the nineteenth century, 'slop shops' had become well established (Wilson and Taylor 1989: 33). The Napoleonic Wars (1793–1815) stimulated growth in government contracts for cheap army or navy clothing. Middlemen employed workers, mainly women, to mass-produce garments in their own homes or in workshops for very little pay (Rendall 1990: 29). The Leeds ready-made clothing industry developed rapidly from the 1860s, where production was divided between the making of trousers (mostly in factories housing early sewing machines, which stitched straight lines only) and of jackets (performed mostly in Jewish workshops by skilled Jewish tailors) (Honeyman 2000: 22).

Many of the early outlets for ready-made clothing enjoyed a far from respectable reputation. Shoddy cloth (made, as we have seen, from recycled wool, cotton, and mixtures from both home and foreign sources) became the staple of the developing ready-to-wear clothing industry. During a period in which a belief in the benefits of recycling was fuelled more by the logic of economics than by either environmental or ethical considerations, the association of shoddy cloth with poor quality must have been at least partly responsible for landing the embryonic ready-to-wear clothing industry with a bad reputation. The nineteenth-century social commentator, Henry Mayhew, was less than complimentary, and contrasted show and slop shops unfavourably with tailoring outlets for bespoke (individually ordered) clothing:

> At the show and slop shops every art and trick that scheming can devise or avarice suggest, is displayed to attract the notice of the passer-by, and filch the customer from another. The quiet, unobtrusive place of business of the old-fashioned tailor is transformed into the flashy palace of the grasping tradesman. Every article in the window is ticketed – the price cut down to the quick – books of crude, bold verses are thrust in your hands, or thrown into your carriage window – the panels of every omnibus are plastered with showy placards, telling you how Messrs —— defy competition. (Thompson and Yeo 1971: 236)

A similar attitude is well illustrated by Arnold Bennett in his novel *The Old Wives' Tale* (1908). By the end of the novel, set in the first decade of the twentieth century, the former drapery store in the Staffordshire pottery town of Bursley (Burslem) has been taken over by the Midland Clothiers Company and is selling ready-made coats. Not only does the way in which the shop advertises itself shock the residents of the town, but the cheapness of the coats constitutes formidable competition to those still in the business of bespoke tailoring. The following extract illustrates something of the provincial conservatism in dress and shopping habits and the antipathy towards ready-made clothing at the beginning of the twentieth century:

> The tailoring of the world was loudly and coarsely defied to equal the value of those overcoats … Twelve-and-sixpenny overcoats! It was monstrous, and equally monstrous was the gullibility of the people. How could an overcoat at twelve and sixpence[17] be 'good'? She [Constance] remembered the overcoats made and sold in the shop in the time of her father and her husband, overcoats of which the inconvenience was that they would not wear out! The Midland, for Constance, was not a trading concern, but something between a cheap-jack and a circus. (Bennett 1908: 4, Ch. 5, III)

Clearly, the kind of entrenched opposition that any business embarking on the ready-to wear venture would need to overcome was considerable. The attitudes described in Bennett's novel reflect the way in which the association with poor quality gave the ready-to-wear industry the dubious reputation it suffered for so long. Considered from this perspective, therefore, the emphasis placed by Marks & Spencer on the provision of quality clothing at reasonable prices suggests the way in which the company must have had to consider carefully the attitudes of its potential customers and how it could overcome ingrained prejudices about ready-made clothing.

Two of the best-known firms catering for the ready-made clothing trade were Elias Moses & Son Ltd of Aldgate and Minories (established in 1834), and Hyam & Company (originally from Colchester, Essex). Both families were originally second-hand clothes dealers with links to the ready-made tailoring trade and established themselves in the City of London before opening West End branches. As well as fashionable off-the-peg garments for men who wanted the clothing opportunities enjoyed by higher social classes, they supplied uniforms, servants' liveries, workwear, outfits for emigrants, mourning clothes and some women's clothing (Breward, Ehrman and Evans 2004: 32–3).

In the mid- to late nineteenth century, the ready-made clothing industry for women lagged behind that for men. Women's underwear could be bought ready-made from as early as the 1840s, although it was, for the most part, stitched by hand well into the twentieth century. The earliest wholesale mantle manufactory in the City of London is thought to have been D. Nicholson of King William Street in 1837. Even before this, however, it was possible to buy part-made dresses, which the customer's own dressmakers could finish to fit (Adburgham 1981 [1964]: 123). Wilson and Taylor (1989: 36) point out that part-made bodices were for sale as early as the 1830s. However, manufacturers did not really start to explore the full potential of ready-to-wear clothing for women until the 1870s (Breward, Ehrman and Evans 2004: 37). In her pioneering work on the history of mourning dress, Lou Taylor has shown how the provision of clothing by well-known mourning warehouses such as Jay's in Regent Street, London, 'encouraged the development of ready-to-wear clothes for middle- and upper-class clients' and that by 1910, completely ready-made dresses were available (Taylor 1983: 192–3). Indeed, by the end of the nineteenth century, certain areas of the ready-made clothing industry were flourishing.

One of the key factors in the development of the ready-to-wear clothing industry during the second half of the nineteenth century was the introduction of a viable sewing machine that could be applied to large-scale factory production. Although the earliest known patent for a sewing machine was granted in 1790 to Thomas Saint, a London cabinet-maker, it is probable that Saint never actually constructed a machine and that his theoretical drawings, translated into a machine, would not have been viable (Beazley 1973: 55). However, a large number of the developments in sewing machines which were to have a major impact on the clothing industry were pioneered in the USA: between 1842 and 1895, a staggering 7,339 patents on sewing machines and accessories were issued (Kidwell and Christman 1974: 75). The first really practical sewing machine was patented by Elias Howe in Boston in 1846, a machine which, however, produced a lockstitch only. Some years later, in 1851, Isaac Merrit Singer introduced a sewing machine from the USA into Britain, developing (in 1854) a machine with a continuous stitch and forward cloth-feed, a mechanism that earlier machines had lacked.

The first entirely machine-made dresses were probably made in the home. However, in the 1850s and 1860s, factories were beginning to house the new sewing machines: it was probably John Barran's famous clothing factory in Leeds – where the clothing trade was one of the most advanced in the country – which was the first factory to use the sewing machine in about 1856 (Adburgham 1981: 128). In the 1840s, Barran had two workshops producing both bespoke and some ready-made garments. In the 1850s, however, he opened his first factory in Alfred Street, Leeds, producing ready-to-wear garments. By 1867 he had moved to larger premises, with stock to the value of £10,000;[18] and by this date almost all the stock was ready-made (Fraser 1981: 177). In these factories, the sewing machines were linked to a central shaft that provided steam power. By the 1870s, gas – and subsequently electricity – was used as the source of power. In other areas of the industry, innovations were also taking place. For example, the introduction of a buttonholing machine and, in 1875, a button-sewer, quickened the pace at which tailoring tasks could be carried out. On the other hand, these innovations did not increase the number of garment pieces that could be worked on simultaneously and it was only with the introduction of the steam-powered cutting knife in the 1870s that machinists could be supplied with the requisite quantities of cut-out pieces, thus significantly speeding up the production process (Leopold 1992: 104–5).[19]

Notwithstanding the importance of technical innovation (the sewing machine and the cutting knife or 'band knife' in particular) in facilitating the growth of the ready-to-wear clothing industry, subsequently the development of the industry relied on increasing labour intensification, especially the exploitation of female labour (ibid.: 108). In 1891, for example, women comprised 70–80 per cent of the Leeds clothing workforce. Machining formed the bulk of women's work, but other 'female' tasks included binding, trimming, buttonholing and finishing (ibid.: 172–3). According to the census of 1881, after domestic service and textiles, the clothing trades occupied the largest single category of paid work for women, mostly in workshops or in their own homes on an outwork basis (John 1985: 37). In fact, for many years, the clothing trade – as distinct from the textile industry, which was heavily mechanized – probably relied more on the supply of cheap and plentiful labour than on technology.

THE WHOLESALE BESPOKE TRADE

From around 1900, large-scale production of ready-made suits was augmented by the manufacture of wholesale bespoke suits – made-to-measure suits that could be sold at the same price as their ready-made equivalent (Honeyman 2000: 2). From the mid-1880s, both Joseph Hepworth & Sons and William Blackburn (established 1867) began to sell ready-made and made-to-measure through their own retail outlets. Honeyman observes that David Little was perhaps the first company to recognize the potential of developing a 'special measure'/'special order' department, whereby customers' measurements and their selection of cloth were conveyed to one of the factories or workshops of the large wholesale companies for making up (ibid.). Like Michael Marks, Meshe David Osinsky (born 1885) was an immigrant and pedlar (of flannel suits). Having first opened a hosiery and drapery shop in Chesterfield in 1904, Montague Burton – as he now called himself – entered the bespoke trade in 1906 (Sigsworth 1990: 34). Advertising in the *Derbyshire Times* in 1906 (14 April), men's suits were 'noted for hard wear and perfect fit (prices from 11s 9d)[20] and boys' suits 'in endless variety' retailed from 1s 9d[21] (Sigsworth 1990: 14).

The distinguishing feature of the multiple tailors, as they became known, was the integration of the manufacturing and retailing of men's tailored outerwear. They opened networks of shops supplied by their own factory production (Honeyman 2000: 55). The Leeds tailors, especially the multiples, observes Honeyman, 'played a key role in extending the social and geographical distribution of men's tailored outerwear' (ibid.: 53). 'For the first time' she argues, 'ordinary working people could afford to buy new tailored woollen clothing comparable with that worn by the middle and upper class' (ibid.). Like Marks & Spencer, it was in the inter-war period that the multiples really expanded, providing in this period 'about a third of all tailored clothing for British men' (ibid.), to the extent that they came to dominate the high street. By 1939, Montague Burton Ltd owned nearly 600 shops (ibid.: 59), taking over from Hepworth, who prior to the First World War had been the largest manufacturer and distributor of men's clothes (ibid.: 65). During this period, the relatively small number of firms producing womenswear, such as Heaton & Co. (established 1900), were also successful (ibid.: 81).

Mort (1997) argues, however, that the clothing multiples such as Burton's, and the wholesale bespoke trade in general, continued to imitate the aristocratic protocols of the genuine bespoke tailors of Savile Row in their approach to customers: 'Burton's suits were factory-made, employing strictly standardized procedures, but 'sir' was measured by Burton's salesmen with all the ritual of a traditional tailoring establishment.' The firm's emphasis, argues Mort, was as much on continuity and tradition as on innovation (Mort 1997: 19). It could be argued that Burton and other retailers of wholesale bespoke suits therefore aligned themselves more easily with traditional taste and retailing practices rather than have to overcome ingrained prejudices.

While the wholesale bespoke trade in men's clothing and its retailing via outlets such as Burton's and Hepworth provide a useful point of comparison with the retail practices of Marks & Spencer, Fine and Leopold argue that the early arrival of mass production and marketing of men's clothing derives less from the tradition of bespoke tailoring than from the early ready-to-wear markets (in the late eighteenth century) for cheap work clothes (discussed above) for those without direct or indirect access to tailoring services, for example sailors, slaves, indentured servants, domestic servants and those building the nation's infrastructure – the navvies (builders of canals and subsequently railways) (Fine and Leopold 1993: 232). What Marks & Spencer was doing in the 1920s lies somewhere in between this tradition and that of the wholesale bespoke trade. On one hand, it was catering for working-class, poor (but employed) people. (Interestingly, the early checking lists show that the company was selling both female domestic servants' uniforms as well as men's work dungarees, for example.) On the other hand, while not initially in the same league as, say, Burton's and Hepworth, Marks & Spencer was also attempting to make its clothing accessible (both in terms of price and the diversity of styles) and respectable (via the company's emphasis on quality).

MARKS & SPENCER AND CHANGES IN THE CONSUMER MARKET IN THE INTER-WAR PERIOD

The nature of women's clothing in the late nineteenth and early twentieth centuries, and the variety of styles that could be deemed 'fashionable' as opposed to the relative uniformity of the male suit, helps to explain in part the slow pace at which mass production could be adopted for the manufacture of female clothing. While the mass-produced male suit has been seen as an emblem of mass society, projecting an image of both cultural democracy and collective masculine uniformity (Mort 1997: 18), women's fashions were more diverse. The fashions of the 1920s, however, were more ideally suited to mass production: the loose-fitting styles associated with the period after the First World War were relatively easy to cut, construct and, significantly, size. Furthermore, fashionable, lightweight fabrics such as silk jersey could be simulated in rayon for a fraction of the price (Breward, Ehrman and Evans 2004: 90). In this context, therefore, the achievements of both the menswear multiples and those retailers such as Marks & Spencer, which pioneered in particular the provision of ready-made women's clothing, constitute major landmarks in the history of fashion.

By the end of the nineteenth century, it was increasingly recognized that those drawing factory wages, in spite of often appalling living conditions, were beginning to experience an improved standard of living, quantitatively, if not always qualitatively, with more disposable income as a result. Hamish Fraser has shown that, on the whole, the higher the income, the greater the proportion spent on clothing (Fraser 1981: 58). However, although working-class incomes rose in the last two decades of the nineteenth century, they did not rise as quickly in the early twentieth century (ibid.: 132). In the 1920s and 1930s there was still desperate poverty. Nevertheless, despite high unemployment, trends towards mass consumerism were becoming apparent during this period and the spending power of those who remained in work was actually increasing, due to a fall in the cost of living. By 1939, according to Wilson and Taylor, the cost of living was 11 per cent lower than in 1924, while average wage rates were 3.5 per cent higher (Wilson and Taylor 1989: 77). This perhaps helps to explain how Marks & Spencer was able to maintain the five-shilling maximum up until 1939.

Furthermore, after the First World War, changing social structures and work patterns meant that middle-class women in particular had less time for fittings, so that high-quality, ready-to-wear clothing became desirable for better-off women as well as for working-class women. The need for quality ready-made clothing was thus a feature of the 1920s and 1930s across all classes. Not only was this a formative period for chain-store expansion into clothing, making ready-made clothing available to working-class people, but it was also the heyday of London department stores in terms of their physical and corporate expansion. Catering largely for the middle market, Debenhams bought Marshall & Snelgrove in 1919, for example, and 1924 saw the opening of Selfridges' western extension, thus providing 14,163 sq. metres (3.5 acres) of floor space in the basement alone (Breward, Ehrman and Evans 2004: 87). Breward suggests ways in which, during the 1920s and 1930s, the visible signs of class distinction were disappearing; that there was a 'flattening out' of differences between the dress codes of the various classes in London and that dress itself was becoming a class leveller (ibid.: 102).

Nevertheless, the impact on patterns of retailing made by the department stores both within and outside London was to make fashionable clothing more accessible to a *middle-class* clientele. However, these stores were still out of the reach of most working-class men and women. Meanwhile, ready-made clothing became especially important for women on low incomes for whom work required smart clothing, but for whom long hours combined with family commitments imposed severe time constraints, making it increasingly difficult to find time to make their own clothes. This was precisely the (huge) gap in the market that Marks & Spencer aimed to fill. To be able to buy ready-made clothing thus became an aspiration and not just a necessity. Daisy Ward (born *c*.1911) recalls working in a Leicester hosiery factory in the late 1920s and 1930s, and describes a ten-hour working day with no lunch breaks or tea breaks: 'I used to go to Marks & Spencer's and get a nice skirt in the old days, it was nothing over five shillings in Marks & Spencer's. For ten shillings I was very well dressed …' (Bowles and Kirrane 1990: 36).

Interestingly, companies which later in the twentieth century would become associated with the retailing of cheap, mass fashion, such as C&A, were selling clothing at substantially higher prices than Marks & Spencer was when it began to sell clothing on a large scale in the mid-1920s. In 1922, the Oxford Street store of C&A Modes celebrated its opening by advertising its merchandise as constituting 'the height of fashion at the lowest cost' (*Evening News*, 4 December 1922). During the 1920s, advertisements for C&A appear alongside (on a full-page spread) those for other department stores: Selfridges (W1), Whiteley's (W2), Derry & Toms (W8) and Bon Marché, Brixton (SW9), for example (*Daily Mail*, 21 August 1922). It would therefore appear that at this time C&A aspired to see its customers in the same middle-class social 'set' as those of its more established competitors. Marks & Spencer, on the other hand, clearly began as a provider of working-class clothing and only later in the century managed to become a repository of middle-class respectability, casting aside an earlier reputation that had placed it on the same level as Woolworth.

It is useful to compare Marks & Spencer prices in the 1920s with those of its 'competitor', C&A, for example. At Marks & Spencer, no clothing in the period 1924–39 cost more than 5*s*. In 1922, C&A was advertising a 'serviceable serge coat' at 15*s* 11*d* (*Daily Chronicle*, 25 September 1922) – more than three times the highest Marks & Spencer price point. This point about the working-class market catered for by Marks & Spencer at this time is confirmed by research into another source: the Hodson Shop Dress Collection, a very rare collection of nearly 3,000 items of 1920s clothing surviving from the stock of a small shop in the town of Willenhall, West Midlands (Taylor 2002: 52–3). The clothing sold from this shop was priced, in the late 1920s, *from* 4*s* 11*d* (this was the price for the cheapest 'tub' or washing-frocks), but the majority of the clothes were much more expensive and out of the reach of factory girls (ibid.: 53). The *upper* price limit at Marks & Spencer, therefore, was the same as the *lowest* at the Hodson shop.

In terms of Marks & Spencer's contribution to the provision of goods for working-class people, the company can be seen in some respects in the same tradition as chains such as Lipton's and the Co-operative retail outlets, rather than in the tradition of the department stores, the latter's clientele being principally middle class. However, other sectors of the retailing industry, which produced goods consumed by a predominantly working-class market, were more advanced than the ready-made clothing industries. This was the case especially in the sector of grocery provision.[22]

Co-operative retailing had flourished in the second half of the nineteenth century, especially in the towns of the industrial north. As already discussed, analysis of Marks & Spencer's checking lists in the late 1930s reveals an astonishing variety of clothes sold by the company in this period. Examples of 'staple ranges' constituted, for example, underwear (locknit and interlock as opposed to the more 'glamorous' artificial silk and, even more desirable, real silk); hosiery; overalls and traditional bib and braces. The popularity of the latter reflects the working-class status of those who bought them. In these lines of 'workwear', Marks & Spencer's main competitors were the Co-ops, which, in 1938, were selling one-third of the total supply of women's and children's clothes, consisting mainly of staple items such as women's underwear and overalls (Wilson and Taylor 1989: 95).[23] But what set Marks & Spencer apart from the Co-ops was that as well as providing basic ranges of clothing, the company also sold ranges that were intended to offer fashion to the working-class customer. For example, in 1938 the company sold new designs in underwear such as French knickers alongside the decidedly less glamorous Directoire knickers (the latter had legs gathered on elastic just above the knee).

As we have seen, following the establishment of Marks & Spencer as a public company in 1926, and the introduction of the 5s price limit, there was also a major rationalization of the goods sold by the company. Furthermore, haberdashery, which from the very beginning had been such an important staple of the company's trade, finally disappeared in 1936. The lists of goods extant for the years 1918 and 1938 respectively reveal a massive transformation in the products sold by the company within these twenty years. The sheer variety of goods sold in 1918 is striking – everything from jampot covers, carbolic soap, suspenders, stationery, skipping ropes, blancmange powder, fuller's earth, Epsom salts, bone shirt buttons, eggcups, metal polish, black lead, not to mention all kinds of haberdashery. When compared with the 1938 checking lists, the latter reveal the extent to which the company had prioritized clothing by this date. In his memoirs, Israel Sieff recalls how, between 1925 and 1940, the growth of the sale of textiles was the 'greatest single feature in this great fifteen-year period of growth … By 1940, textiles had become the biggest single section of the company's business, at least three times as large as any other' (I. Sieff 1970: 145).

Michael Marks had always kept a keen eye on which of his products were selling and which were not. Simon Marks continued this tradition, both via the information gleaned from the checking lists but also at first hand. Whenever he visited a store he would, reputedly, obtain sales information by asking the sales assistants questions about the merchandise that was selling best. The importance of monitoring past and current sales and trialling new lines came to play a vitally important part in determining future Marks & Spencer buying policy. Thus, it became part of the company's normal procedure to test a sample of merchandise before selling it on a large scale and thus integrating it into the bulk ranges. As Rees explains:

> When new lines were introduced, it was possible, with the cooperation of suppliers, for a sample range to be offered for sale in a limited number of stores, and in this way Marks & Spencer used their counters as a kind of laboratory for testing demand … In this rapidly changing picture, the greatest single factor was the growth of the company's range of textiles. They covered a wide range, including hosiery and knitted goods, gloves, overalls and dresses, tailored shirts, pyjamas, nightwear and socks.' (Rees 1973: 141)

By the eve of the Second World War, textiles represented the largest section of the company's business. Meanwhile, the decision to abandon the sale of haberdashery in the mid-1930s was clearly significant: not only was it recognition that this was no longer a profitable or appropriate line of business for the company but, in a broader context, it was an indication that people were no longer making their own clothes to the same extent as they had done in the past, and that the market for ready-made clothes was reaching maturity. Marks & Spencer, Burton's and C&A, for example, had not only responded to this new demand, but helped to create it. Indeed, by 1925, Montague Burton's 'new' clothing factory, situated in Hudson Road, Leeds, was reputed to be the largest clothing factory in Europe, servicing by far the largest chain of textile stores in the world (Sigsworth 1990: 54).

The inter-war years witnessed massive expansion of the total number of Burton's shops, fuelled partly (in the immediate aftermath of the First World War) by the demand for made-to-measure suits during the demobilization of 1918–19 (40 shops in 1919; 60 in 1920; almost 600 in 1939) (ibid.: 41). Equally, the sheer physical expansion of Marks & Spencer during the latter part of this period is impressive: between March 1927 and March 1939, the number of stores increased from 126 to 234. By the mid-1930s, Marks & Spencer was represented in every town of any considerable size throughout the country (Rees 1973: 96) and was shaping the look of the high street. Buying procedures were becoming increasingly centralized. In 1920, Simon Marks had moved to London from Manchester. After moving to various London addresses, Marks & Spencer's head office (Michael House) moved to 72–82 Baker Street in 1931 and remained there until 1958, when it moved to 47–67 Baker Street.

It is significant that Marks & Spencer's corporate expansion went hand in hand with the evolution of the retailing of clothing. By 1928, the company had established its own brand name for the goods manufactured to its own specifications – St Michael. Initially, the St Michael brand name (Fig. 6) was applied to a strictly

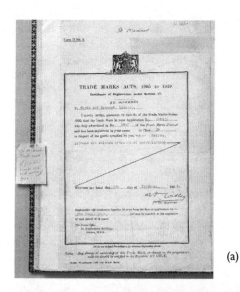

6: (a) Registration of the St Michael trademark, 5 November 1928 and (b) St Michael trade-mark, 1932.

limited range of Marks & Spencer products – shirts, pyjamas and knitted articles of clothing, with mackintoshes following in 1931. The St Michael brand name became a guarantee of the quality of the product it was selling. The pursuit of 'quality' became crucial to the success of Marks & Spencer in order for its policies to result in the disassociation of ready-made with 'shoddy', especially significant within the largely unexploited context of the mass production and consumption of clothing for working women and working-class women. From the 1930s, this became possible through the company's approach to the technological and design processes in the production of the merchandise it would retail, considered in the following two chapters.

> We put the technologist behind the retail counter, and once you start selling
> quality, and quality control, there is no limit.
>
> Israel Sieff[1]

> Large-scale production for a mass consumer market needs safeguards to ensure
> that the merchandise is of the highest possible quality consistent with the price
> policy.
>
> Ismar Glasman to Simon Marks, memo, 4 Novemeber 1953

Fashion as currently understood would not exist without technological innovation. In the twentieth century, developments in fabric and clothing technology have helped to define and to change fashion. Without the employment of technology, the individual design is an unrealized dream: technological improvements and expertise make it a reality. Moreover, when clothing is produced on a large scale, the role of technology – including everything from the development of new fabrics with easy-care qualities, the monitoring of fabric performance and the provision of a garment-sizing and grading system, to colour coordination and standardization – becomes absolutely vital in order to ensure uniform quality. For children's clothing in particular, the role of technology is vital to ensure safety (the non-flammability of fabrics and the importance of securely attaching buttons, for example). For the majority of people, fashion is therefore not just about the style of a garment, but about how that garment fits the body, how it feels next to the skin, how it washes and wears, and how it performs in relation to the other garments being worn with it. For example, while in the 1950s a woman's slip may have been a glamour garment in its own right, it becomes less desirable if it clings, irritatingly and uncomfortably, to the dress or skirt worn over it. Clothing also becomes less attractive to the consumer, if, when taken out of the store environment, it changes colour in daylight (it is metameric) to the extent that it cannot be worn with the supposedly coordinating garment it seemed to match in the shop. These factors are so critical to the creation of a successful range of garments that it is difficult to imagine a time when they could not be taken for granted.

This chapter will examine the impact of the company's involvement with technology (defined in the broadest terms), arguing that Marks & Spencer's reputation as a retailer of quality clothing was established by placing technology and design at the centre of its retailing philosophy (Worth 1999: 234–50). Commenting on the company's success in the shoe sector in 1995, former joint managing director Andrew (now Lord) Stone, underlined the importance of the roles of technology and design: 'Innovation of *technology* and *design* has been key,' he asserted (*Draper's Record*, 27 May 1995: 8). Indeed, it is no coincidence that the textile laboratory, merchandise development department and design department (see Chapter 3) were all established in rapid succession in the 1930s.

THE IMPORTANCE OF RESEARCH

> The role of technology in Marks & Spencer is the application of knowledge to the development and production of our merchandise … we should be innovators, which, by definition, means the commercial exploitation of a new idea from whatever source. (David Sieff, 20 October 1981)[2]

Recognition of the vital role that continuous technological research and innovation played in pioneering what was essentially a new industry in the 1920s and 1930s was implicit in the company philosophy which Simon Marks and Israel Sieff were formulating during this period. It was no coincidence that Simon Marks visited the USA in the 1920s, and that his trip consisted primarily of research into the development of the retailing and ready-to-wear clothing industries. Significantly, the one American retailer Simon referred to by name in his notes was Sewell Avery, chairman of the company Montgomery Ward (Bookbinder 1993: 90).

Founded in 1872, Montgomery Ward initiated the principle of selling exclusively by mail, in order to tap the huge potential market of small-town residents and farmers. Although initially there was a much bigger volume of men's and boy's clothing than of women's (in 1875 its catalogue offered more than 135 pages of men's garments and only 26 pages of 'ladies' skirts and underwear' and 'hoop skirts and corsets'), by 1920, of the 872 illustrated pages of the spring/summer catalogue, 25 pages were devoted to men's and boy's wear and an impressive 84 pages to women's ready-made clothing (Kidwell and Christman 1974: 161). In the 1920s, it expanded extraordinarily rapidly and began to operate retail stores as well: by the end of 1927 it had thirty-six stores and by 1931, this figure had risen to 610 stores (Lebhar 1952: 325). For Simon Marks's fact-finding mission, therefore, the fact that by the 1920s, the company was a substantial supplier of women's ready-made clothing and a retailer as well, was significant. Furthermore, on a later business trip, Avery advised Simon on the role of *technology* in obtaining the correct goods.

Specifically, however, it is probable that sizing systems were of great interest to Simon Marks, especially since this factor – in particular for women's clothing – constituted a considerable stumbling block for the progress of the women's ready-to-wear clothing industry. During the American Civil War, the chest and height measurements of over a million conscripts were taken, providing for the first time a mass of statistical data regarding the form and build of the American male. This was compiled into a table of proportions. Although the study was helpful as a guide to the industry, it omitted many important dimensions (Kidwell and Christman 1974: 103). (For women there was no compilation of female statistics corresponding in scale to this one.) Nevertheless, as early as 1875, Montgomery Ward promised the following: 'Give your age and describe your general build, and we will in nine cases out of ten give you a fit.' Men were offered coats, vests and overcoats in sizes running from 34–40 inches, trousers in sizes 30–36 inches. By 1879, there was also a special section devoted to extra-large clothing for men (ibid.: 105). In spite of the fact that there was a proliferation of sizes offered by the ready-to-wear clothing industry in the USA and no real common standard under which these sizes were determined, Montgomery Ward's system must have been one of the most advanced in terms of sizing technology and it is significant, with regard to the aspirations of Simon Marks for Marks & Spencer in the 1920s, that he made special mention of this company.

Apart from the research Simon Marks did into the American ready-to-wear clothing and retailing industries, Marks & Spencer has a long history of founding and supporting textile research institutes, from the foundation of the Daniel Sieff Research Institute at Rehovot in Israel in 1933 (in memory of Israel and Rebecca Sieff's son) to the establishment of the Weizmann Institute in 1946. The Weizmann Institute was named after the industrial chemist and Zionist leader Chaim Weizmann, a friend of Simon Marks and Israel Sieff from their Manchester days. When Israel Sieff first met him in 1913, Weizmann was working at Manchester University as a lecturer in industrial chemistry and the friends were united by their mutual interest in the Zionist cause. Of significance to the history of Marks & Spencer was the fact that Weizmann later impressed upon Simon Marks and Israel Sieff the importance of the role of technology to the company. Indeed, Israel Sieff observes that Weizmann advised the company on the potential of man-made fibres long before they were an actuality (I. Sieff 1970: 147). Under Weizmann's influence, explains Sieff, 'We came to regard ourselves as a kind of technical laboratory … We learned to exercise an active influence on production generally, and on the textile industry in particular' (ibid.). Both the terms in which Sieff describes the company and the fact that Marks & Spencer, a retailer, aimed to make an impact on the process of production and thereby on the textile industry, are significant (see below).

From the 1930s, Marks & Spencer subscribed to and supported a number of research associations for the clothing industries.[3] For example, in 1936 the company subscribed to WIRA (Wool Industries Research Association) and maintained a close link with the SHIRLEY Institute (Cotton, Silk and Man-made Fibres Research Association). In its pursuit of quality merchandise, Marks & Spencer recognized the value of such research bodies as advisory agents. For example, prior to subscribing in 1954 to SATRA (British Shoe and Allied Trades Research Association), Marks &

Spencer sent samples of all its children's shoes and sandals to the association's laboratory in Kettering for examination, as part of a conscious policy of upgrading its children's footwear. Those lines of merchandise that SATRA found fault with were withdrawn (*St Michael News*, April 1954: 1). Soon after, Marks & Spencer subscribed to SATRA.

Simon Marks set up Marks & Spencer's own formal research arm in 1943 – the merchandising development research committee – which was linked to the merchandise development department (see below).

MARKS & SPENCER'S RELATIONSHIP WITH ITS SUPPLIERS

In 1926, the year that Marks & Spencer became a public company, Israel Sieff became a full-time director, thus bringing his considerable experience of the textile industry to the company. One of Israel Sieff's early achievements was his reappraisal of the traditional relationship the retailer had with the supplier, and by implication, the retailers' involvement with the production of the merchandise it would sell (already mentioned above). While the wholesale bespoke trade relied on the retailer having ultimate control over production because it was also the manufacturer (Burton's, for example, maintained control over the manufacture of the clothing it sold until the early 1980s, when it closed the majority of its manufacturing bases and focused on retailing), it was otherwise unusual for retailers to take such a 'hands-on approach' to the processes of production. Moreover, up until the 1920s at least, after which time its importance was declining, the Wholesale Textile Association had played an important 'go-between' role, effectively preventing direct trading between the retailer and the manufacturer, thereby distancing any reciprocal relationship – beneficial or otherwise – between the two. The persuasive arguments Israel Sieff used to convince the hosiery supplier Corah of Leicester to deal directly with Marks & Spencer resulted in the wholesaler being bypassed altogether. Sieff believed that if Marks & Spencer was to ensure the retailing of high-quality garments at lower prices, dealing directly with the manufacturer was essential.

In 1910, Marks & Spencer had investigated the possibility of reducing costs by manufacturing for itself a proportion of the merchandise sold by the company. The failure of these attempts highlighted for Marks & Spencer that the specific roles played by manufacturer and retailer were essentially different. As Bookbinder observes, 'The failure of these ventures established a company principle of not dabbling in areas outside its established sphere of excellence', thus making the advice of Michael Marks particularly relevant: 'You either make things or you sell them. Don't try both!' (quoted in Bookbinder 1993: 62). On the other hand, although the company divested itself of the ultimate responsibility of manufacturing, it became uniquely involved with all aspects of the production process, from research into yarns and fabrics, the implementation by suppliers of new machinery, and the minutiae of the various stages of the production process. According to Lewis Goodman, Marks

& Spencer became 'a manufacturer without the machinery' (Interview with Lewis Goodman, 26 January 1999; see note 13).

Cutting out the wholesaler and dealing directly with suppliers facilitated negotiation between Marks & Spencer and its suppliers on the price and quality – and later design – of the products to be sold in stores, rather than allowing the retailer to be presented with a 'fait accompli' range of goods by its suppliers to be selected by the buyer. Not only did this process have the potential to directly reduce the unit price of garments, but it had a significant impact on the products sold and gave the retailer a significant level of responsibility for the look and the quality of clothing on the sales floor. It also imparted to the Marks & Spencer buyer, working closely with the technologist and merchandiser, a significant role in the creation of garment ranges and would, in effect, set the company apart from its competitors in this respect.

Thus, Marks & Spencer's pioneering work in the field of technological innovation and fabric development would not have been possible without the direct relationships which the company forged with its suppliers over the years, from the early years when Michael Marks purchased his goods for peddling from Dewhirst, a policy continued by Tom Spencer, who also bought direct from the manufacturer (Bookbinder 1993: 37). Later, when Israel Sieff persuaded Corah of Leicester to deal directly with Marks & Spencer in the late 1920s, Sieff's motivation was not only to avoid the wholesaler and reduce costs but was also a way of facilitating long production runs in order to increase overall profits. Furthermore, he wanted to make it possible to plough more money back into – and thereby improve – the product. By cutting out the wholesaler, manufacturer and retailer could communicate and hence make clothes to Marks & Spencer's specifications: on a practical level, this set up a dialogue between Marks & Spencer's own textile experts and those of its suppliers. The benefits passed on to the customer were perceived by Marks & Spencer in terms of offering better *value*, that is, the best quality at the best price. The St Michael brand (registered in 1928) was to become a guarantee to the customer that any article that carried it had been subjected to strict methods of quality control at every stage in its manufacture. It thus became associated with 'quality', which became the hallmark of the products sold by the company.

For Marks & Spencer, 'quality' implied controlling the sources of production in order to ensure that the high standards imposed were met. Over time, and as the number of stores increased, the quantities of garments Marks & Spencer could sell also increased. Depending on the production capacity of a particular supplier, the same style of garment might be – and frequently was – manufactured across more than one supplier. In order to ensure standardization of production, therefore, Marks & Spencer had to lay down specifications that applied to all suppliers producing that style. What came to be relationships of mutual dependence between manufacturer and supplier were formalized in 1947 when Marks & Spencer set up a factory organization section – later known as the production engineering department – which was designed to assist manufacturers in the progressive modernization of their plant, and enable them to adapt to the latest technological advances (Briggs 1984: 67). A number of booklets published by the production engineering department survive in the Marks & Spencer Archive. These booklets gave suppliers detailed guidance on the make-up, finishing and general quality expected from garments manufactured to Marks & Spencer's specifications. Later, in 1973, the industrial management group was set up to help and advise suppliers on a range of issues, not least in the areas of technology, engineering, administration, staff management and welfare. Clearly, Marks & Spencer perceived its relationship with its suppliers to be a reciprocal one. As one contributor to *St Michael News* in 1954 commented (the patronizing tone was probably unintentional but is nonetheless telling), 'We learn as much from the skills and experiences of our suppliers as they from us, perhaps more (*St Michael News*, 17 December 1954: 3).

From the point of view of the manufacturer, the long production runs offered by Marks & Spencer, as well as the possibility of cooperation in terms of shared expertise and investment in new machinery, also proved attractive. In the 1990s, however, there was harsh criticism of the fact that some suppliers manufactured for Marks & Spencer exclusively – or, in the case of large companies such as Courtaulds and Coats Viyella, that Marks & Spencer was by far their biggest customer – and that suppliers were therefore 'vulnerable' to the 'whims' of the retailing 'giant' (*Draper's Record*, 30 March 1996: 12).[4] The Dewhirst Group, for example, supplied Marks & Spencer exclusively in the mid-1990s. However, the association with Marks & Spencer of more than a hundred years' duration was regarded by some as positive.[5] The fierce competition on the high street both during this period and subsequently, clearly put pressure on both retailers and suppliers and it would be naive to lay 'blame' solely at the doors of the retailer.

'THE FIRST PRACTICAL STEP IN THE EVOLUTION OF TEXTILE TECHNOLOGY'

> The approach taken by Marks & Spencer in the procurement of merchandise is fundamental to our future success. It is essential that the use and laboratory testing of garments form an integral part of the buying process, so maintaining the differential of quality between ourselves and our competitors.[6]

In 1935, Marks & Spencer took the unusual step of establishing its own in-house textile laboratory (Fig. 7) with the aim of improving the quality of fabrics to be used in Marks & Spencer garments, thereby enabling company technologists to specify in detail to the manufacturers the fabric quality they wanted (Bookbinder 1993: 101). As Ismar Glasman, former director of technology, pointed out in 1981, 'It was the first practical step in the evolution of textile technology.'[7] The idea of a textile laboratory, according to Mr Glasman, was highly innovative, Selfridges being the only other store

7: Marks & Spencer's textile laboratory, head office, late 1930s.

to have one, although the latter was rather different in purpose, because it dealt only with customer returns.[8] Marks & Spencer's textile laboratory became a venue for subjecting fabrics to tests of washability and durability and between 1935 and 1939, no fewer than 9,000 such tests were carried out. The results showed that the qualities of fabric used for some of the core Marks & Spencer clothing ranges were uneven. This resulted in the establishment of the merchandise development department in 1936, which had the specific task of improving the quality of Marks & Spencer merchandise.[9] 'Here', explained Israel Sieff, 'we tested for colourfastness and shrinkage, the character of yarns and dyeing processes, and probed into the problems of the production of textiles by modern mass-production methods' (I. Sieff 1970: 156).

Marks & Spencer invested carefully in its specialist personnel. The merchandise development department was put under the direction of the highly gifted industrial scientist and expert in textile technology, Dr Eric Kann, who had joined the company in 1935. Responsible for many of the pre-war improvements in clothing standards at

Marks & Spencer, Kann also conceived the idea of a separate design department (see Chapter 3). This would be significant for future company philosophy with regard to the interdependence of high quality and good design in clothing (Worth 1999: 234–50). In 1939, Marks & Spencer also recruited Eric Heim to its merchandise development department, another textile specialist originally from Vienna and previously managing director of a textile company near Prague.

THE IMPACT OF THE SECOND WORLD WAR

The contribution made by Marks & Spencer to the democratization of fashion is a dominant theme of this study, and the impact of the Second World War needs to be assessed in the light of this process. The role of technological development in the fashion industry at this time became a necessity in the context of wartime exigencies. In terms of dress, it can reasonably be argued that government-led initiatives such as clothes rationing and the Utility clothing scheme broke down some of the traditional class divisions in the consumption of clothing. Clothes rationing, for example, meant that whatever your level of income, and unless you were able to get hold of coupons via the 'black market' (which some people inevitably did), you were limited in your acquisition of clothing by a fixed (for all income brackets) number of clothing coupons per year. Furthermore, it may be argued that the Utility scheme effectively ensured that clothes conceived by well-known designers became available to all classes and not just to those in higher income brackets.

During the 1930s, Marks & Spencer had already begun the process of making reasonably priced, quality clothes available to a growing sector of the population. The in-house *Marks & Spencer Magazine* in 1932 (15–17) includes an article entitled 'How to Get Two Pounds' Worth for a Pound: Mrs Goodwife Goes Out Shopping'! (Fig. 8) The tellingly named Mrs Goodwife is given £1^{10} by her husband, and manages to buy essential items for her wardrobe. Her husband is so impressed that he gives her another £2 to buy clothes for the children and, finally, he goes to buy an outfit for himself. The aim of the article, of course, was to promote the ways in which Marks & Spencer clothing offered exceptional value for money via the provision of quality merchandise at affordable prices. In so doing, the company clearly perceived its role in terms of contributing to higher living standards. In 1936, Simon Marks told the shareholders:

> Goods and services once regarded as luxuries have become conventional comforts and are now almost decreed necessities. A fundamental change in people's habits has been brought about. Millions are enjoying a substantially higher standard of living. To this substantial rise in the standard of living our company claims to have made a definite contribution. (quoted in Briggs 1984: 45)

On the eve of the Second World War, the company had 234 stores and a total of 71 km (44 miles) of countering, with no single item costing more than 5*s* (Bookbinder

8: 'How to Get Two Pounds' Worth for a Pound: Mrs Goodwife Goes Out Shopping', *Marks & Spencer Magazine*, Summer 1932.

1993: 114). The effect of the war was double-edged. There was the human cost in terms of serious staff casualties amongst those serving in the British armed forces and, in addition, substantial store damage. Marks & Spencer's simple pricing structure was also disrupted by war. Not only was the 5s limit abandoned, but the 1939 Prices of Goods Act required individual pricing for each size of children's socks. Following negotiations with the government, however, Marks & Spencer was permitted to average the price of virtually identical articles, which helped the company to simplify its price structure once again (Bookbinder 1989: 48). There were also shortages of clothing caused by rationing and the Utility scheme, and clothing suppliers clearly had difficulties in supplying Marks & Spencer with the requisite goods. Some suppliers had to change to producing goods specifically for the war effort. For example, the majority of the supplier Clifford Williams's production of men's and boys' trousers was converted to the daily manufacture of 1,200 sets of army battledress tops plus 600 trenchcoats (Bookbinder 1989: 134). After 1941, Marks & Spencer's turnover and profits showed a sharp decline, as the following figures illustrate:

Year ending 31 March	Total turnover (£000)	Textiles and fancy goods (£000)
1938	20,015	16,031
1941	29,132	21,358
1945	18,104	12,562
1948	34,104	23,267

Source: Bookbinder 1989: 139.

Rationing and shortages were still very much in evidence in the years after the war. Indeed, as the figures show, it was not until the late 1940s that Marks & Spencer achieved pre-war turnover levels. On the other hand, the impact of clothes rationing and the Utility scheme was largely beneficial in so far as its long-term effect on the process of democratization was concerned.

The government's system of clothes rationing was formally introduced in 1941 and lasted until 1949. Clothing could only be bought with coupons and while the allowance was initially sixty-six coupons a year in spring 1942, this was reduced to sixty for fifteen months (approximately forty-eight coupons a year) due to increasing shortages (Wilson and Taylor 1989: 116). Wilson and Taylor have shown that by 1941, the British were spending 38 per cent less on clothes than in 1939 (ibid.: 110). They point out that during the Second World War, although class differences persisted, it was unfashionable to look wealthy (ibid.: 113). Because of rationing, people had to make clothes last – although this was hardly a new challenge for poor families – and they must therefore have chosen the few clothes they did buy for their quality and value. This factor, allied with the 'fashion' for a style that had less to do with looking opulent than maintaining a smart appearance with the minimum of effort, must have given the clothes being sold by Marks & Spencer a greater appeal than hitherto.

The Utility clothing scheme was formally introduced in 1942, although it was conceived the previous year. Like rationing, it was the result of wartime shortages, and was intended to regulate the amount of fabric used for garments as well as to limit unnecessary trimmings, buttons and so on. Thus, 'unnecessary' turn-ups on men's trousers, for example, were prohibited. Although the original Utility garments were designed by well-known couturiers, Utility clothing was subsequently made at every price level, from couture to mail order (Wilson and Taylor, 1989: 120). Based as they were on designer prototypes but produced at different price levels, it can be argued that Utility clothing gave everyone – in theory at least – access to well-designed clothes.

At Marks & Spencer, Utility clothes contributed to the greater part of the company's turnover in clothing during this period and the company appears to have benefited from the Utility clothing scheme (Briggs 1984: 55). A large number of Marks & Spencer Utility-specification garments survive – with the familiar CC41 (Civilian Clothing, 1941) label – including rayon St Michael Utility stockings and a man's shirt (Fig. 9) and a Utility housecoat with the St Margaret label (attached to those garments made by Corah of Leicester). The specifications for the manufacture of clothing under the Utility scheme drew widely on Marks & Spencer's knowledge and experience, making use of its staff in applying and administering the scheme (Rees 1973: 162). Specifically, Marks & Spencer technologists cooperated with government scientists in devising Utility specifications.[11] Bookbinder explains how, in 1941, many of the standards formulated by Marks & Spencer during the 1930s for basic clothing materials, trimmings and garment manufacture were utilized by the government, with Marks & Spencer playing an important role in helping the Board of Trade to determine standards for Utility clothing. One of these fabrics, recalls Lewis Goodman, was Utility Schedule 1005, an extremely successful spun viscose fabric, later known as Marspun (Interview with Lewis Goodman, 26 January 1999) (see Chapter 3). Marks & Spencer textile technologist Harry Atkinson worked with Harold Wilson at the Board of Trade to determine standards for Utility clothing, as well as advising on the correct allocation of clothing coupons (Bookbinder 1989: 45). One of the consequences of the Utility scheme and of clothes rationing was to encourage customers to be more discriminating in their choice of clothes by demanding better quality, more hard-wearing garments. Equally, manufacturers probably took more care in their choice of materials and paid more attention to their standards of garment make-up. Potentially, one of the most important consequences of the Utility scheme was to improve and extend good design so that it would be within the reach of all (Wilson and Taylor 1989: 125).

The government's 'Make Do and Mend' campaign probably had more impact on the well-off, who had never, out of sheer necessity, had to prolong a garment's life by

9: (a) St Michael CC41 Utility rayon stockings and (b) Utility men's shirt, Marks & Spencer Archive.

mending it, even though they may have done so for reasons of economy. To the poor, on the other hand, who had always mended their clothes, the Make Do and Mend directives must have appeared patronizing to say the least. Apart from the repercussions of the government's rationing measures and Utility scheme in regulating clothing production and consumption, the Concentration scheme, which began in

1942, also had the effect of rationalizing the British clothing industry. Under the scheme, the government permitted a limited number of existing clothing factories to continue production and this had the effect of eliminating some manufacturers at the bottom end of the market. The result was often better-quality garments, produced by manufacturers on whom greater demands were being made by more discerning customers.

Therefore, in spite of the short-term disruption caused by war, the effects on both the clothing industry as a whole, and on the Marks & Spencer clothing product in particular, were to contribute much to the democratization of fashion in the long term. In a number of ways, the war accelerated scientific and technological progress in the textile and clothing industries. In 1943, Simon Marks set up a merchandising development research committee at Marks & Spencer, whose terms of reference were 'to assist the company in planning for post-war [development] by keeping abreast of the scientific and technical developments in industry and agriculture, [and to] provide a link between the company and research institutes' (Bookbinder 1989: 114). By 1945, the merchandise development department was publishing a series called *Textile Bulletin*, which looked prophetically to the future, with the aim of providing information regarding 'practical developments which are taking place and which are likely to be of interest to us [Marks & Spencer] … Trade papers carry stories of the wonders of nylon, plastics and all the other materials which may revolutionize our lives. But from this mass of information it is often difficult to extract the wheat from the chaff; to know what should be disregarded and what should be taken seriously.'[12]

After the Second World War, a new textile testing laboratory was opened in 1946. When the Utility scheme ended in 1952, the merchandise development department split into three sections: cloth buying, colour and print, and technology. This was clearly an indication that each area had specialized tasks and was also an illustration of the expanding and increasingly sophisticated role performed by technology throughout the business, as well as the growth of the company per se. For example, the cloth buying department, under the leadership of Eric Kann, was specifically responsible for sourcing fabrics, processing orders and monitoring the quality of the cloth, ensuring that the appropriate cloth was available at the right time for the manufacturers (*St Michael News*, April 1960: 7).

In practical terms, the application of technological knowledge and expertise to the development of the Marks & Spencer clothing product went hand in hand with the aspiration for better quality merchandise. For example, there were a number of improvements to basic ranges in the early 1950s, imperceptible no doubt to the customer at the time of purchase, but which contributed much to the longevity of that garment's life: for example, the introduction of nylon 'splicing' in men's wool socks in 1953, making them much more hard-wearing (*St Michael News*, June 1953: 1). In the manufacture of slippers, the development of the 'vulcanization' process (the bonding of a rubber sole to a slipper upper at intense heat and under pressure) gave greater durability and comfort as well as a non-skid tread (*St Michael News*, August 1953 'Slipper Special': 1). In men's knitwear, details such as ribbon backing for the buttons and buttonholes on cardigans were important in the quest for continuous improvement of the product.

In fact, in the 1950s and 1960s, knitwear was one of the most progressive sectors of the business, both in terms of technological and fashionable innovation: for example, in the late 1950s, Marks & Spencer adopted the use of double yarn for knitwear as opposed to using 'singles' yarn. Double yarn results in a jumper or cardigan of much better quality which, when washed, retains its shape; whereas a garment knitted from singles (single-ply) yarn tends towards 'spirality' when washed, with the result that the garment loses its pristine shape and side seams sit in the wrong position on the body. These examples illustrate the ways in which the company was deliberately trying to distinguish itself from its competitors by developing superior products in quality terms (*St Michael News*, June 1953: 2).

THE DEVELOPMENT OF NEW FABRICS AND THE IMPORTANCE OF EASY-CARE CLOTHING

> Man-made fibres have undoubtedly made an enormous contribution to improving the standard of life of millions of men and women, to reducing the burden of household drudgery, and to creating new articles of clothing which meet the needs and tastes of our times. What the consumer wants to buy is clothing which is at once light and warm, and easy to wear and care for and meets the increasing tendency towards informal living. These new conceptions of clothing are an integral part of a social revolution which is changing all our ways of living. (Eric Kann, 1 May 1962)

Eric Kann neatly sums up the ways in which, by the 1960s, the needs of the customer had changed in favour of practical, casual and easy-care clothing and the contribution that new (man-made and synthetic) fabrics had made in responding to this demand. In the period after the Second World War, one of the most important preoccupations of Marks & Spencer technologists was the introduction of new, commercially viable fabrics for use in Marks & Spencer garments. A number of textile dictionaries (produced principally for the use of employees) survive in the Marks & Spencer Archive and provide some telling insights into the changing priorities the company had in terms of new fabrics. For example, *Facts about Fabrics* (1954), complete with useful swatches of the fabrics it describes, is filled predominantly with information about cotton, wool, rayon and nylon. The commercial viability of the newer synthetics – the polyesters and the acrylics still lay in the future. Twenty years on, however, in a textile dictionary for 1975, the importance of the polyesters and acrylics is unequivocal and the revolutionary fabric, Lycra (first introduced at Marks & Spencer in the early 1960s for use in corsetry) is very much in evidence by this date.

From the 1950s, one of the motivations behind the introduction of new fabrics at Marks & Spencer, and in the textile industry generally, was an awareness of changing economic factors and shifts in consumer demand. As living standards improved, observed Eric Kann, and as the world population continued to increase, there was a greater demand for more and better-quality clothing (Kann, 1 May 1962, Marks & Spencer Archive). According to an optimistic writer for *St Michael News*, more goods would 'become the right of everyone' (*St Michael News*, 3 December 1954: 2). By the early 1960s, according to Kann, although the growth of synthetic fibre production had been dramatic, that of wool and cotton had trebled (Kann, 1 May 1962, Marks & Spencer Archive). However, natural fabrics such as cotton, linen and wool were seen to be exhaustible and the advantages of man-made and synthetic alternatives lay in their reduced price *potential* and easy-care qualities. At the company's annual general meeting in 1964, Simon Marks reported that more than half of Marks & Spencer's textile sales were now in garments made from man-made and synthetic fibres. Including blends (with natural fabrics) the proportion was nearly two-thirds (Goode, May 1965, Marks & Spencer Archive). Marks & Spencer clearly aspired to be at the cutting edge of these new developments. In a paper presented to the Textile Technology Symposium in 1969, Ismar Glasman described how, 'through our technological strength, we [Marks & Spencer] were able to introduce these fabrics [the nylons and the acrylics] into our merchandise at a far greater pace than anybody else' (Glasman, November 1969, Marks & Spencer Archive).

It is useful to compare the dates when the new fabrics became available and the dates on which Marks & Spencer began to sell them. The hosiery potential for nylon (produced by the American company Du Pont), for example, was first announced in October 1938. However, wartime scarcity meant that even when nylon finally appeared in Britain after the war, there were signs in shop windows saying: 'Only available to foreign visitors' (Handley 1999: 50). In an article for *St Michael News*, Marks & Spencer described how S. & J. Deyong Ltd (suppliers to Marks & Spencer since 1934) obtained the first available supplies of warp-knitted nylon after the Second World War, producing nylon waist slips for Marks & Spencer (*St Michael News*, February 1972: 5). Nylon stockings were also sold by the company shortly after the war (*c*.1947) and a large range of nylon lingerie followed (Fig. 10). By the late 1950s–1960 the company was selling nylon goods produced by British Nylon Spinners, who in 1958 had introduced its own brand name Bri-Nylon (Handley 1999: 72). In particular, it was the easy-care qualities of nylon that were important to Marks & Spencer, as the following observation in *St Michael News* illustrates:

> Today, a girl simply takes a handful of detergent in the bowl, whisks the whole lot – slip, nightdress, briefs, bra and girdle – through the suds, gives them one rinse and lets them drip-dry. That's the drill in millions of homes where there's St Michael Bri-Nylon lingerie. (*St Michael News*, November 1960: 4)

10: Window display of St Michael nylon lingerie, Edinburgh store, 1957.

Orlon, originally called 'Fibre A', was another of Du Pont's 'easy-living fibres' and was first announced in 1949 (Handley 1999: 70). With its remarkable capacity to form a staple fibre, thereby creating the bulkiness of wool, Orlon uniforms were described in the *Du Pont Magazine* as early as 1952 and this acrylic fabric was being sold only six years later at Marks & Spencer (probably by 1958) (Fig. 11). The first British acrylic fibre – Courtelle – was produced by Courtaulds and first introduced in the mid-1950s; it was trialled by Marks & Spencer in 1960 (Fig. 12).

Since its introduction to the Marks & Spencer customer in about 1954 (following the lifting of British clothing restrictions in 1952), one of the most successful of the synthetic fabrics for Marks & Spencer to date has been polyester. The first public announcement of ICI's brand, Terylene, was placed in the

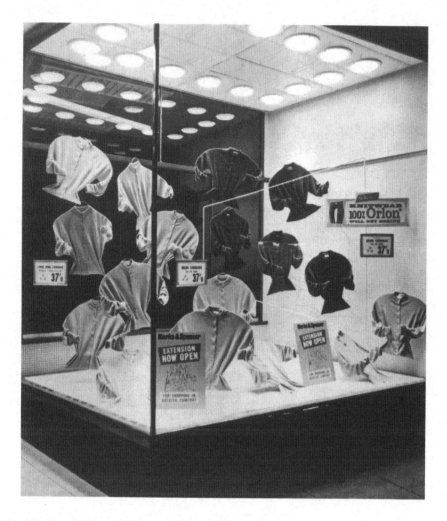

11: Window display of St Michael Orlon knitwear, 1950s.

Manchester Guardian on 5 October 1946. Along with Du Pont's Dacron, this fabric would soon command vast world markets (Handley 1999: 55). 'Crease resisting', washable, permanently pleated sun-ray skirts made of Terylene (sometimes mixed with wool) and Terylene trousers for men (Figs 1 and 13) combined easy-care qualities with smart, popular fashion. The popularity of Crimplene, both at Marks & Spencer (Fig. 14) and in the British clothing market generally, was more short-lived. Marks & Spencer was selling Crimplene by the mid-1960s. Although, as Handley points out, many people took it to be a completely new fabric, it was actually just another form of polyester developed by ICI in 1955: its uniqueness lay in the fact that it had been 'crimped' (ibid.: 114). The man-made fibre triacetate

12: St Michael Courtelle knitwear, *Ambassador Magazine*, 1967.

(better known as Tricel) was marketed both by Courtaulds and British Celanese. Although acetate was first invented in 1914, technical problems with the fibres had prevented their use until the 1950s (ibid.: 68). At Marks & Spencer, it was sold as blouses from about 1957.

In the early years of their development, the new man-made and synthetic fibres were considered primarily as 'substitutes' for natural fibres and were not necessarily invested with an aesthetic value. By the early 1960s, however, according to Ismar Glasman, they were beginning to be seen as important in their own right, with unique benefits, providing the key to offering the customer a better product in terms of performance, colour and price.[13] Israel Sieff observed that the new fabrics gave women the kind of clothes they required at a price they could afford to pay (I. Sieff 1970: 181). Working closely with their suppliers on the development of new fibres (M. Sieff 1988: 234), Marks & Spencer saw itself in the vanguard of 'progress' towards their introduction to the consumer. Of course there was a financial incentive for the company too: before the price wars of the late 1960s (see Conclusion), garments made from synthetic fibres were more expensive than cotton and the more established man-made fibres (rayon), and therefore gave a better return per square foot of selling space (Goode, May 1965, Marks & Spencer Archive). In 1971, an

13: Window display of St Michael men's Terylene trousers, Coventry store, 1957.

analysis of sales by fibre reveals that whereas sales of natural fabrics had increased from £62,440,000 in 1966 to £73,175,000 in 1970, sales of man-made and synthetic fabrics (nylon; polyesters; acrylics and rayons) had risen from £116,100,000 to £191,025,000 in the same period (Anon., 2 February 1971, Marks & Spencer Archive).

Marks & Spencer's enthusiasm for the introduction of new fabrics in the 1950s was clearly influenced by a deliberate policy of making 'the housewife's burden' a less onerous one. This is well illustrated in Simon Marks's 'Christmas Greetings' to Marks & Spencer employees in December 1958: 'Not only do they [nylon, Orlon, Terylene and Tricel] provide attractive garments,' he pointed out, 'but they also have the advantage of easing the housewife's daily burden' (*St Michael News*, December 1958: 1). 'Increasingly too it [St Michael] is becoming a symbol of easier living … The lot of many a housewife has been lightened by St Michael drip-dry and easy to launder garments …' (ibid.: 4).

14: Twiggy wearing a St Michael Crimplene dress, *Ambassador Magazine*, 1967.

Hand in hand with the development of easy-care fabrics was the increasing consumption of labour-saving devices for the home. Historian Elizabeth Roberts observes that to have an electric iron in the home was usual by 1960, while 3.6 per cent of families nationally had washing machines in 1942, compared with 64 per cent by 1969 (Roberts 1995: 29). However, the arrival of the latter did not necessarily mean that women spent less time on domestic chores (ibid.: 33). Mass Observation, for example, reported in 1961 that suburban London housewives spent a staggering seventy-one hours per week on domestic activities (ibid.: 30).

In spite of the undisputed enthusiasm in the post-war period for man-made and synthetic fabrics and their easy-care qualities, they did not replace natural fabrics. In fact, in the 1950s, when British cotton firms were being hit by foreign competition and exports were declining, Marks & Spencer aimed to promote the cotton industry by highlighting the fact that 99 per cent of the cotton cloth sold in Marks & Spencer stores was spun, woven and finished in Britain (*St Michael News*, September 1958: 4). *St Michael News* also reported how some of the earliest experiments (*c.*1937) in bringing about standardization in finishing and dyeing undertaken by Marks & Spencer were done in conjunction with firms manufacturing cotton (*St Michael News*, 25 February 1955: 1).

Furthermore, even as Marks & Spencer was concentrating on the development of the new synthetics, the company also focused its technological expertise on giving natural fabrics easy-care qualities. For example, in the 1950s a new resin finish was applied to cotton used for dresses, allowing the fabric to be drip dried with very little ironing necessary (*St Michael News*, 3 August 1956: 4). Another method of producing an easy-care, drip-dry fabric requiring the minimum of ironing was to mix cotton with the new synthetics (*St Michael News*, April 1957: 3). Of these developments, one of the most important was that of machine-washable wool – Marks & Spencer playing a leading role in developing this process. From the early 1950s, all St Michael knitwear had been made shrink-resistant (the development of machine-washable wool would depend heavily on a successful shrink-resist treatment) so that it could be safely washed by hand (*St Michael News*, November 1972: 1). By the mid-1960s, a two-ply yarn for a harder-wearing fabric and the application of a special shrink-resist treatment made lambswool and Shetland wool increasingly popular for men's and women's knitwear. The development of machine-washable botany wool was followed closely by the announcement of Marks & Spencer's first machine-washable lambswool and Shetland wool garments in 1972.

Along with these breakthroughs, the company published information about caring for clothes. Leaflets distributed to customers, such as one in 1974 entitled 'How to Take Care of Your Clothes', not only offered advice to customers regarding washing particular fabrics but also introduced customers to the new care symbols for washing, bleaching, ironing and dry-cleaning, which were made compulsory on labels (*St Michael News*, July 1974: 3).

While some synthetic fabrics – such as nylon and Lycra, as well as some of the polyesters and acrylics – were definitely here to stay, the popularity of certain fabrics such as Crimplene and Tricel proved to be short-lived. From the late 1980s, (in the 1990s in particular), there was a resurgence in the popularity of natural fabrics, marketed in particular for their luxurious feel and appearance. Once again, there was an emphasis on giving them easy-care qualities. Machine-washable silk is an excellent example of this. The success of non-iron cotton, first in menswear and then in the late 1990s in womenswear, also reflects the increasing demand for fabrics which look smart but are casual, but which at the same time require the minimum of care. Likewise, the 1987 appearance in menswear of machine-washable suits (70 per cent polyester and 30 per cent wool, with a polyester lining) (*St Michael News*, May 1987: 5), and then in womenswear in the mid-1990s, was an indication of changing lifestyles and of the increasing demands made upon men and women in terms of juggling their work and domestic roles. In summary, the developments in easy-care fabrics reflected the need to maintain a smart appearance with only the minimum of time and effort. In the 1990s (with the development of entirely new fabrics such as Microfibre, Tactel and Tencel) as in the 1950s, the development and introduction of new fabrics lay at the heart of the company's pursuit of wearable and popular fashion.[14]

QUALITY ISSUES AND FABRIC PERFORMANCE

One of the central concerns of the technology teams at Marks & Spencer was consistently to improve the quality of fabric and garment performance. Unpublished papers (mainly correspondence between Marks & Spencer technologists and those at the company's suppliers) at the Marks & Spencer Archive reveal the minutiae of technical experimentation: how, for example, technologists in the late 1970s endeavoured to find an anti-static solution to apply to nylon knitted fabric for women's slips, and to secure high-specification standards for the zips used on Marks & Spencer garments. In departments such as children's schoolwear, the performance of the fabric used became a priority for Marks & Spencer in the 1950s: gabardine used for children's coats and mackintoshes underwent stringent tests for permeability to water (*St Michael News*, July 1954: 2). In the early 1960s, Marks & Spencer announced a 'revolutionary new treatment for rainwear' – Scotchguard – which enabled rainwear to be dry-cleaned without damaging the proofing (*St Michael News*, Autumn 1961: 2). In the late 1970s and early 1980s, Marks & Spencer was again striving to improve 'rainproofness' in ranges of adult rainwear, following tests conducted by the 'rain simulator' in the textile laboratory which revealed that water was penetrating the seams of garments as a result of the type of sewing thread used. In addition, in the 1950s, Marks & Spencer technologists concentrated on developing various shrink-resistant processes for staple garments such as socks (*St Michael News*, June 1953: 3). By the 1970s, the 'Sanforized Shrunk' trademark was being used on Marks &

Spencer garments, denoting that any garment which carried the trademark conformed to a quality standard of shrinkage control. As already discussed, a successful shrink-resist process was essential to the pioneering of fabrics that could be machine-washed, in particular knitwear.

Colourfastness (colours that do not run when washed or wet) also became an important element in establishing the company's reputation for quality. In the early 1950s, 'vat-dyeing' for many of Marks & Spencer's garments, including men's shirts and pyjamas, was thought to be the best method of obtaining a good level of colour-fastness (*St Michael News*, October 1953: 3–4). The company aimed to match or exceed the very highest standards laid down by the industry, as the following example illustrates. In the late 1960s, Marks & Spencer introduced a new standard on St Michael nylon underwear fabrics: approximately thirty different shades were colour-fast when washed at 60°C, explaining: 'That is about ten degrees warmer than anyone would want to wash nylon at … This raises the standard to ISO3, the highest practical standard for washing nylon issued by the International Standards Organization' (*St Michael News*, December 1967: 6).

In order to monitor the quality of the clothing sold by Marks & Spencer, the company set stringent standards of quality control, with inspection taking place at different stages of garment manufacture as well as in stores (Fig. 15). In 1974, the quality monitor was set up and was run by the industrial management group from

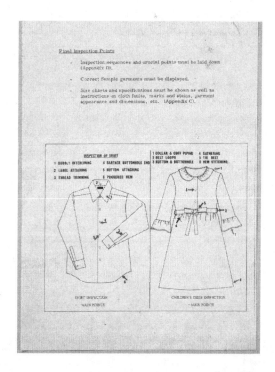

15: 'Final Inspection Points', guidelines for manufacturers produced by the production engineering department, 1970s.

the Oxford Street Pantheon store.[15] The purpose of the quality monitor was to identify any faulty merchandise before it found its way on to the sales floor and then to display it at the quality monitor room at head office. Merchandise from each of the different departments was then analysed on a rota basis (*St Michael News*, March 1978: 2). The principle of monitoring the quality of goods, both at the point of manufacture and in the stores, became a measure by which the quality of merchandise was gauged. As a sort of postscript to this section, the author recalls that (while on the Marks & Spencer graduate training scheme for selectors, 1990–91) the customer service department at head office would give 'goodwill' refunds to customers who, for example, returned a jumper after literally years of wear, complaining that it was wearing out. It would be difficult to find another retailer who rewarded its customers for expecting this level of quality.

SIZING

As discussed in Chapter 1, the development of a reliable and sophisticated sizing system was one of the key factors upon which the development of the ready-to-wear clothing system in Britain depended. Badly fitting clothes had given the industry a reputation for poor-quality products. From the late 1920s, more sophisticated American sizing methods were frequently used by companies producing ready-made clothing. For example, Olive O' Neill, designer for the well-known and high-quality ready-to-wear company, Dorville, dissatisfied with the existing British standards of manufacture and, above all, with sizing, adopted American methods of sizing, grading and manufacture in the 1930s (Ewing 1993: 130).

Not surprisingly, Marks & Spencer also utilized American sizing as the prototype for its grading system (*St Michael News*, February 1957: 1). In the 1950s, the company also tried to simplify sizing: for example, a 36-inch hip became a size 12 while a 50-inch hip became a size 26 (ibid.). Carried out by the research department, one of the first size surveys conducted by Marks & Spencer, 'A Scientific Approach to Stocking Sizes', took place in 1957. At this time, stocking sizing was largely a matter of guesswork, and although a number of surveys had been conducted within the industry, surprisingly none of the existing measurement surveys of women had included both leg *and* foot measurements. Although the sample for the survey at Marks & Spencer consisted of just a cross-section of employees, and was obviously limited to measuring only the lower body, this was an important step in the quest for a more scientific approach to the complex issue of sizing. As a result of the survey – which showed that six out of ten women apparently bought the wrong-size stockings – a new range of 'superfit tailored nylons' went into production. These were fully fashioned, resulting in no wrinkling around the ankles, and no trouble with seams riding round (*St Michael News*, September 1957: 1).

In the 1950s there were also a number of attempts to make special ranges for those women whose figures did not fit into the 'average' size statistics. For example, in 1953

Marks & Spencer announced a new range for the 'shorter woman' (defined as being under 1.57 m/5 ft 2 in) (*St Michael News*, June 1953: 1). A wide selection of skirts in this range was introduced in July 1954, accompanied by showcards and other publicity to display in stores. At the other end of the spectrum, just a few years later, thirty stores received the 'first-ever' range of dresses in cotton and Marspun (see Chapter 3) for women of above-average height (1.75 m–1.8 m/5 ft 9 in–5 ft 11 in) (*St Michael News*, June 1957: 1). In the same year, the company developed a range for the 'fuller figure'. Thirty years on, Marks & Spencer announced the launch of a 'plus' range, catering for women of up to size 24 (*St Michael News*, May 1987: 3). The range was not an unqualified success, however. Following this, a 'plus' range for men was launched in five stores (*St Michael News*, April 1988: 2) and in the mid-1990s, there were womenswear trials of sizes 22 and 24, in a selection of eighty different garments, to be sold in selected stores in the north and the Midlands (*St Michael News*, March 1995: 8). Rather more successful, at least initially, was a range of maternity wear, introduced into selected stores at about the same time (*St Michael News*, August 1987: 1). These developments are interesting as they reveal the difficulties of gearing mass production towards anything but 'average' sizes, and the continuous attempts by the company to extend its customer range.

Until 1988, Marks & Spencer's general sizing for women (other than for stocking sizes) was based largely upon a survey conducted by the Board of Trade in 1951. By the 1980s, and no doubt long overdue, came the recognition that the height and body curves of women had changed over the preceding thirty years, due to such social factors as the keep-fit boom, different nutrition, the contraceptive pill and the large-scale shedding of heavyweight corsets and bras. In 1988, a survey was undertaken in association with Loughborough University and with the participation of ten Marks & Spencer suppliers. It involved more than 6,000 women aged between seventeen and sixty-nine, at thirty-one stores. The results were published in 1989 and revealed that the 'average' British woman was 1.62 m (5 ft 4 in) tall, i.e. 2.5 cm (1 in) taller than thirty years previously. Although waist and bust measurements were filling out, Marks & Spencer concluded (somewhat tautologically) that its existing size 14 (the retailer's biggest seller) 'coincides within millimetres with the size 14 shopper out there' (*The M&S Magazine*, Spring 1989: 63). As a result of the survey, a new size 10 was introduced, which was more generous, thus enabling the company to introduce what it described as a 'meaningful size 8' (*St Michael News*, September 1990: 3).

The first major size survey for men was undertaken in 1984, and for boys in 1979, the latter also in association with Loughborough University. Before this date, there was virtually no data for British boys. As the preface to the survey indicated, the situation was less critical for girls because of standards laid down by BS 3728, which was based on a survey done in the USA before the Second World War, marginally updated in the mid-1960s. It was not until twenty years later, however (1986), that a major survey for girls was carried out. Establishing criteria for the sizing of children's wear and babywear has always been complex. In 1960, a new and simplified 'sizing by age' method was announced for all children's clothes (*St Michael News*, February 1960: 1). By 1979, however, this system had been abolished, partly as a result of the preliminary findings of the boys' size survey.[16] Subsequently, age once again became the guiding criterion for sizing, although measurements were also given on the labelling of babies' and children's clothing.

In August 1996, *Draper's Record* reported that Loughborough University was again working with Marks & Spencer and its suppliers on new methods of research into sizing. The university survey involved 200 adult women and looked mainly at bra sizes. While the 1989 survey discussed above had used traditional methods, the 1996 project team used a machine called the Loughborough Anthropometric Body Scanner. The article described how the scanner shines across the body while it rotates, and in eleven minutes can take coordinates for the whole body. The shape is then entered into the computer for use in CAD (computer-aided design) programs and manufacturing. This initiated more widespread, critical research into sizing within the retail industry in general, including that carried out by the Burton Group and Oasis for example (*Draper's Record*, 10 August 1996: 5).

THE ROLE OF COLOUR TECHNOLOGY

> Colour is the most important factor in promoting sales. (Ismar Glasman, 18 September 1981)

The necessity for establishing colour standardization across a business as large as the one Marks & Spencer had become by the 1950s would probably be lost on today's customers, precisely because it is so much taken for granted. Nevertheless, it is imperative that different suppliers of the same or coordinating ranges of garments adhere to particular colour standards and that the garments manufactured do not vary noticeably in colour. Only when a rack of skirts vary slightly in colour when they are, in fact, supposed to be exactly the same does colour standardization become a significant quality issue. It is even more unacceptable if the customer buys one of these skirts along with a supposedly matching top and subsequently discovers that the two garments are slightly different or, worse still, clashing in shade when s/he takes them out of the bag to admire them, either in the street or at home, and finds that the colours vary in daylight and tungsten or fluorescent lighting respectively.

Significantly, following a detailed discussion in the company's colour room in 1958, regarding the need for coordination between allied buying departments with regard to the standardization of basic colours, a consensus was finally reached.[17] The priority would be to avoid clashing colours and it fell to Ismar Glasman (see Note 7) to provide the necessary liaison between different departments in order to bring this about. It was resolved that a colour library of woven fabrics would be built up alongside the colour library already created for the knitwear group (which had pioneered the task of colour standardization). The result was the Marks & Spencer Colour Bank, a collection of all the colour samples for different fabrics used in garment ranges from the mid-1950s (Fig. 16).

The principle of colour standardization – that there had to be specified standards and tolerances of shades of colour to which all Marks & Spencer buying departments and suppliers must adhere – was well established therefore by the end of the 1950s. Ismar Glasman recalls how, early in the decade, Patons & Baldwins (a principal supplier of knitwear to Marks & Spencer at the time) met with Marks & Spencer technologists, under the direction of John Ingham (then head of the textile technical services team) and established the principle of colour standardization. Following this, swatches of yarn were sent to different dyers and knitters to use as colour standards. This meant that all suppliers and Marks & Spencer personnel had to subscribe to a particular shade of, for example, the colour red, which would then be common for that particular fabric across the business, irrespective of the dyer or fabric supplier. Because different fabrics take dyes differently, there was likely to be some variation between each type, but the importance of establishing a colour

16: Ismar Glasman working in the colour room, head office, 1960s.

standard was that the degree of variation was monitored and only a certain degree of tolerance permitted.

A breakthrough in colour matching was made in the early 1980s with the installation of a computerized system whereby the colour of a fabric sample could be measured and precise tolerances stipulated. This system – developed by the British company Instrumental Colour Systems (ICS) working jointly with Marks & Spencer – made possible the sale of men's (and subsequently women's) suits as separate jackets and trousers or skirts, where it is absolutely essential to have exact colour matching (*St Michael News*, April 1981: 7). In 1984, the Queen's Award for Technology was awarded jointly to ICS and Marks & Spencer as a result of this breakthrough.

Colour standardization was also driven by aesthetic considerations, such as achieving a 'good black' or a 'good navy', although this is a subjective process to some extent and is partly dependent on the type of fabric being dyed. Simon Marks clearly had high standards with regard to colour. For example, Ismar Glasman recalls how, in the mid-1950s, he was asked to do a presentation to the chairman on colour coordination (Interview with I. Glasman, 20 January 1997). Afterwards, he was invited by Simon Marks to the latter's Grosvenor Square house in order to see an 'excellent shade of green' in a pair of *silk velvet* curtains. Such an 'ideal' shade would, presumably, have been rather more difficult to achieve in rayon or nylon, but Mr Glasman's recollection is interesting for the way it illustrates Simon Marks's quest for uncompromisingly high standards.

As Ismar Glasman pointed out to the author in our discussion (Interview with I. Glasman, 20 January 1997), 'You can't have colour standardization without standardizing light conditions.' The principle of light standardization takes as its premise the fact that, to the human eye, colours appear to change according to the light in which they are viewed and that some colours on some fabrics are more 'metameric' (they appear to change colour in different kinds of lighting) than others. At the same time as embarking on colour standardization in the mid-1950s, Mr Glasman observed that Marks & Spencer was the first retailer to standardize lighting. It did this by using a 'special colour-matching unit' to give standardized daylighting throughout the day (*St Michael News*, July 1958: 2). This was followed by the introduction of a light box in which the colours of fabric swatches and garments could be monitored, thereby enabling Marks & Spencer to check that different fabrics used for coordinating ranges of garments did not suddenly appear to clash when placed under different lighting conditions. The light box used by Marks & Spencer and its suppliers from the mid-1960s simulated store lighting, daylight, tungsten and ultraviolet light (*St Michael News*, December 1967: 6). The introduction of the colour box, along with colour standardization, gave the company the potential for the successful retailing of the coordinated separates which became so fashionable in the 1950s and 1960s (see Chapter 3).[18]

> Think of your skirt and sweater in coordinated terms ... take a blue cardigan and match it to a toning blue skirt, then look for a scarf that deepens the whole blue effect and there, madam, you haven't just got a sweater, skirt and scarf ... you've got yourself fashion. (*St Michael News*, May 1961: 2)

The effect of developments in technology as applied to different processes in the mass production of clothing has been to open up fashion to new possibilities. Not only did the evolution of technology contribute to pushing the boundaries of what would define fashion in the second half of the twentieth century, but it has also contributed to its democratization. In childrenswear, for example, experiments in the 1950s with machine-applied embroidery and machine-made broderie anglaise helped to break down the boundaries of privilege associated with the exclusiveness of hand-stitched decoration, thus making these popular fabrics available to everyone.

This chapter has discussed some of the ways in which advances in technology – especially the development of new fabrics – have opened up the possibilities for innovation in fashion. The issues surrounding colour – in particular the standardization of colour and lighting conditions – afford as good an example as any of the interdependence between technology and fashion. One of the first fabrics for which colour standardization was achieved in the 1950s was double jersey, used for the hugely popular ranges of Marks & Spencer jerseywear (Fig. 17 and see Chapter 3). One explanation for the success of the jerseywear ranges is that they were perceived as 'fashionable', at least in part because different pieces could be variously coordinated. Furthermore, the styling was smart and the fabric was easy-care.

The introduction of new 'fashion fabrics' such as Tactel and Tencel in the 1990s illustrates the extent to which change and novelty in fashion continued, in the late twentieth century, to be facilitated via technological breakthroughs. According to an article in *Draper's Record*, Marks & Spencer's attitude to the development and marketing of new fabrics was consistently innovative and the company committed to using the latest technological expertise. Speaking at the 1997 annual Innovation Lecture in London, organized by the Department of Trade and Industry, the Marks & Spencer deputy chairman, Keith Oates, stressed the point that technological innovation would be key to the future of the Marks & Spencer clothing business. In particular, he cited the importance of working with Du Pont on Lycra, a fibre which at the time was incorporated in one-quarter of all Marks & Spencer's clothing sales (*Drapers Record*, 1 March 1997: 7).

The realization that changes in fashion can be achieved through a retailer's active participation in technological innovation lay at the heart of Marks & Spencer's retailing philosophy and the formal recognition of research and experimentation was symbolized, as we have seen, by the establishment of the textile laboratory in 1935.

Grey and white two-way striped collar, and 1953's three-quarter sleeves characterize this blouse. Deep ribbing helps the waist line.

Dolman sleeves are still " in " on this best-selling cardigan which is especially cut to fit over most garments without crushing.

Peg top skirt with a vent in the back for easier movement. Can be worn with any separate blouse or cardigan.

An alternative gored skirt, generously cut with a smooth hip line and full hem. Wide waist band adds character and style.

JERSEY MATES are interchangeable

KEY-NOTE for jersey mates is "inter-changeability." The cardigans, and the blouses, can be worn with any skirt in the range to give a complete and satisfying ensemble.

The aim is to persuade customers into buying a *collection* of jersey mates; several skirts and a selection of blouses and cardigans making a base for various ensembles.

To achieve this, uniformity of design and manufacture becomes increasingly

important. It is good to record that manufacturers have, in fact, co-operated well in ensuring standard quality and finish.

Making a Match

Nevertheless, yarn from different sources may not always be precisely the same finish. To minimise this, the department has arranged that stores will receive matching sets from the same source, and that one maker will operate the same matching set. Where possible, too,

makers of matching sets will get their yarn from the same source.

Colour Important

Colour is important. In addition to the popular and well-established shades of grey, cherry, emerald, gold and purple, new and exciting colours are making their appearance, often for the first time on M. & S. racks.

Graphite is a very dark grey; there's a new lime green, and a variety of effects are being achieved with the basic grey and contrast sleeves. There are some interesting results with knitted contrast edging too.

Sleeve Selection

Cardigans and blouses are available with high, medium or low necks; with three-quarter sleeves or long, set-in or Magyar.

There are twin-sets in jersey too, classically or sportingly styled.

The skirts are pencil, flared and pleated, with individual numbers within the range.

WORLD APPROVED *(from page 1)*

For blouses it is 8 oz. minimum per yard 54 in. wide, and dresses 9 oz. minimum per yard 54 in. wide.

The fabric is now given a special finish for finest worsteds called Decatising.

The jersey range has already achieved considerable publicity in the home and overseas press.

French *Vogue* pictured one of the lines, while *Sunday Express* fashion columnist Drusilla Beyfus ran an M. & S. blouse and skirt in her "Golden Girl of the Shops" feature.

ACROSS THE CHANNEL

Letters of appreciation from all over the world are kept in a file in T.58. They come from as far apart as Northern Rhodesia and New Zealand, Sweden, and, of course, from all parts of this country.

Here's a comment from Belgium : " I was very pleased to be able to find a woollen dress to suit me in your store in Oxford Street ; for, in the Ardennes, where I live, the winters can be very cold.

" I must tell you that I have not seen in Paris or Brussels woollen dresses so finely styled at such a low cost as the one I wear."

17: 'Jersey Mates', *St Michael News*, July 1953.

It is also reflected in the close working relationships nurtured between designers and technologists. The conviction that technology and design must operate *together* for the improvement of clothing ranges became central to the company's retailing strategy. Having discussed the vital role of technology for the Marks & Spencer clothing business, that of design will now be considered.

Our [Marks & Spencer's] position in the ready-to-wear fashion world is very
high, because we do real fashion. Fashion is, after all, the clothes that are worn
by the majority, and by that definition, we are a great influence.

Michael Donéllan, quoted in *St Michael News*, January 1967

Although the history of the clothing sold by Marks & Spencer is not that of high
fashion, it serves, however, as a guide to defining what fashion (as subjective as the
term undoubtedly is) has meant, on a day-to-day basis, to those people for whom the
world of haute couture is little more than an unattainable dream. Although the latest
catwalk couture and ready-to-wear collections have become increasingly accessible via
magazines, newspaper coverage and, increasingly, the Internet, what is presented to the
customer on the high street is ultimately what constitutes fashion for the majority.
This was the view expressed by the couturier Michael (see above) who worked as a
consultant for Marks & Spencer in the 1960s. Indeed, the 'majority' would, in all
probability, eschew the extremes of high fashion even if it were within their budget.
The history of the high street and high-street clothing itself have been influenced by
the development of retail outlets as diverse as the covered market and the department
store in the nineteenth century, the chain stores from the early twentieth century and
the boutique from the 1960s. From the late twentieth century to the present time, it
has been shaped by the growth of clothing outlets as diverse as Jigsaw, Karen Millen
and Monsoon to the relatively inexpensive Peacocks, Primark and Be-Wise, for
example. While companies may define their market according to customer age and
level of income (and increasingly lifestyle), the reality is that customers don't always
'conform' to these categories in the way that marketing companies and retailers might
hope or expect. What has happened is that fashion and the consumption of fashion
have, over the last hundred or so years, undergone a process of democratization,
thereby losing many of their associations with an elite social group and indeed defying
any broader categorization by age, class, status and income.

While the role of Marks & Spencer has to be seen in the broader context of the
development of retailing in general, the company made a specific contribution by
making high-quality, inexpensive clothing available in the UK and subsequently
worldwide. From the perspective of the present, fabrics such as nylon, Marspun, or
Crimplene – the latter predicted by Marks & Spencer to be '*the* high-fashion fabric
of 1967' (*St Michael News*, December 1966: 6) – may not be considered to be

fashionable. Rather, what is considered to be fashionable has, by definition, to be of the moment – be it a style of garment or type of fabric. Our perception of what is fashionable is coloured by more contemporary fabric developments: Lycra from the 1970s, and Tactel and Tencel in the 1990s, for example. It took the return of 1950s twinsets in the 1990s for a younger generation to appreciate that twinsets only became 'frumpy' in the 1970s and 1980s in the eyes of a generation who had worn them in their youth and for whom other fashions had subsequently taken their place. The same could be said of flares. The fact that flares became fashionable again in the 1990s – albeit in a number of different styles, ranging from a wide flare to the very slightly flared 'bootleg' trouser – has, perhaps, enabled the fashion writer to reassess more objectively their impact when they were fashionable the first time around in the 1970s. An appreciation of the transient (and cyclical) nature of many fashions helps the contemporary fashion commentator to revisit the past with a greater degree of objectivity. Therefore, an assessment of the historical contribution made by Marks & Spencer to fashion needs to be made, if possible, without transferring contemporary ideas about what is fashionable on to the past, but rather to consider the fashions of any period in the context of their time.

From the 1930s, Marks & Spencer captured an increasing share of the market in a number of different ways, not least and as we have seen, by giving technological innovation a central role in the development of the clothing ranges. This went hand in hand with investing the design process with the utmost importance, both in-house and within design teams working for the company's suppliers. The result was that rather than suppliers presenting Marks & Spencer with ranges of garments as a fait accompli, employees at Marks & Spencer and their suppliers went through a lengthy process of presentations and debate in which the design and selection of garment ranges were finally accomplished through the Marks & Spencer 'review'. This chapter will consider both the importance of the design process and the relationship between the clothing sold by Marks & Spencer and that deceptively simple but complex term, 'fashion'.

THE DEVELOPMENT OF THE DESIGN DEPARTMENT

Quality clothing is clothing that not only performs well but which is well designed. Of course there is no paradigm for design excellence, but what is significant in any assessment of the Marks & Spencer contribution is the company's recognition, as early as 1936, of the important role of design; a central design department was established at this time (Rees 1973: 147; Briggs 1984: 67; and Fig. 18).[1] This decision reflected the company's desire to keep abreast of the latest trends in fashion and design and to create a team of experts and technicians, whose services would also be available to Marks & Spencer's suppliers. From its inception, Parisian designers were employed and 'standards of taste were added to those of quality' (Salmon 1957: 6, Marks & Spencer Archive). The establishment of the textile laboratory, merchandise

18: Marks & Spencer's design department, head office, late 1930s.

development department (Chapter 2) and then the design department reflected the priority given to the improvement of Marks & Spencer clothing, both in terms of quality *and* design.

The idea of a design department was conceived by the gifted industrial chemist, Dr Eric Kann, who joined the company in 1935 and, as we have seen, became responsible for technology. Important links between the areas of technology and design were thus forged at this early stage, and help to explain the continuing inter-dependence between these two key areas. Individual recollections of past Marks & Spencer personnel illustrate the dialogue that took place between members of the technology and design teams. Technologist Ismar Glasman (see Chapter 2) recalls that he worked closely with Hans Schneider, head of design from 1949 to 1976. For example, they travelled together to Milan in order to research the latest fashion trends.[2]

Not only was a design department established in the 1930s, but it was also during this period that Edward Sieff (younger brother of Israel Sieff) helped to coordinate the work being done in the buying departments. The role of the latter became a key factor in the overall design and buying process. Edward Sieff also developed the concept of the merchandiser working alongside the selector, both with different but related roles (M. Sieff 1988: 226). This distinction between merchandiser and selector was unusual: in many other retailing operations, the role of buyer encompassed that of both merchandiser and selector. At Marks & Spencer, however, the merchandiser would negotiate with the supplier on issues of price and quantities of merchandise, and might try to influence decisions to do with the aesthetics of a range of garments in relation to possible effect on future sales. The selector, meanwhile, was responsible, first and foremost, for the aesthetics of the garment, overseeing the design and, working closely with the technologist, the fit of the garment. The selector's brief would also be to keep abreast of the competition on the high street (during, for example, 'comparative shopping' exercises) and on what the company described as 'forward fashion trends' via 'directional shopping' in the fashion capitals of the world: Paris, Milan, New York and so on.

Before the mid-1980s, the function of the design department was both practical and interpretative: practical because it was here that designs were evolved, the patterns for designs made and size charts prepared; interpretative in so far as it was also the role of the design department to study fashion trends and work with selectors on new ideas. In 1967, for example, it was estimated that while 90 per cent of Marks & Spencer lingerie designs and 75 per cent of skirt designs were produced by the design department, up to 40 per cent of dress designs were submitted by the company's suppliers, some of whom, like Corah of Leicester, had their own design room (*St Michael News*, Autumn 1967: 12). From the mid-1980s, however, the tasks of designing and pattern-cutting were transferred more completely to Marks & Spencer's suppliers and, as the company continued to expand both in the UK and abroad, one of the most important functions of the design department became the coordination of design throughout the business, reflected in the production of the design brief (discussed below).

As early as the 1930s, Simon Marks kept in touch with developments in fashion in London and on the Continent. Harry Sacher recalls that in 1938, Marks & Spencer began the purchase of printed fabric designs from Paris studios: 'The results of this work', he observes, 'were very far-reaching: business could be very much stimulated by the introduction of really genuine designs, produced by a Paris artist' (unpublished history, Ch. VI: 60–1, Marks & Spencer Archive). However, it was during the post-war period that the design department underwent its major development and expansion under the guidance of Hans Schneider, who joined the company in 1949 (M. Sieff 1988: 233). From a total staff of only eight in 1949, by 1953 there were approximately sixty people employed in the design department.[3] A separate print design department was also established after the Second World War in order to advise both the buying departments and Marks & Spencer's suppliers on types, patterns, and colours of prints. Here, original textile designs were evolved and then utilized for appropriate Marks & Spencer clothing ranges (Rees 1973: 182 and I. Sieff 1970: 181). Subsequently, however, Marks & Spencer's suppliers took on the task of sourcing print designs and the final selection of prints was the result of discussion and negotiation between suppliers, Marks & Spencer selectors and the design department.

In the 1950s, Marks & Spencer continued to build contacts with fashion houses on the Continent (Rees 1973: 183). Both in this task and in the overall development of the key role of design at Marks & Spencer, the contribution of the highly creative (and, by all accounts of those who worked with him, volatile) Hans Schneider would be significant. Schneider looked to the top end of fashion for inspiration for the Marks & Spencer clothing ranges. Former Marks & Spencer designer, Richard Lachlan, recalls working under Schneider and going to the Paris couture shows where toiles of the latest designs from the House of Dior, for example, would be bought and subsequently used as the basis for Marks & Spencer designs.[4] According to former director of technology, Lewis Goodman (who joined Marks & Spencer as a technologist in 1947 and worked for the company for thirty years), Schneider's main contribution lay in his 'ability to lead selectors to following up those fashions which were appropriate to the Marks & Spencer business' (Interview, 26 January 1999). This would be accomplished through 'window shopping' and visiting the trade fairs. Ultimately, the most important of such trade fairs would be Première Vision (established in 1973), held in Paris. Such visits by Marks & Spencer designers and selectors would constitute a starting point for the then twice-yearly research process to identify and interpret future international fashion trends and make them appropriate to the requirements of the Marks & Spencer customer.

From its inception, therefore, the aim of the design department was to oversee the role of design throughout the company as a whole, paying particular attention to styling, colour and fabric. From the late 1940s, members of the design team, as well as selectors in the buying departments, studied general fashion trends in order to improve the Marks & Spencer product. To what extent were these influences incorporated into the actual clothing sold by Marks & Spencer? As the analysis in the following sections reveals, the design department endeavoured to make good design a priority in order to improve the quality of Marks & Spencer clothing.

MARKS & SPENCER AND FASHION: THE 1950S AND 1960S

> Marks & Spencer is news, fashion news. Barely a week passes without one magazine or other drawing attention to some line which is on the racks or counters. Proof positive that we are on the right style lines. (*St Michael News*, 3 December 1954: 4)

Thus writes the fashion commentator Mary Welbeck, whose articles in *St Michael News* during the 1950s provide the reader with some fascinating insights into the company's perception of its position with respect to the world of fashion. Not only did the company believe that it was 'on the right style lines', but there is also evidence to suggest that it saw itself in the vanguard of fashion in some respects and that it did in fact 'set the fashion' (Fig. 19).

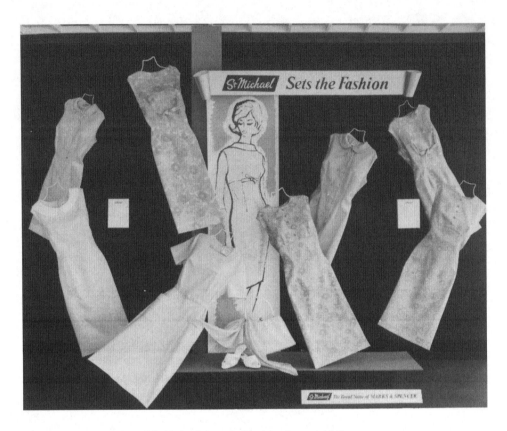

19: Window display of St Michael dresses, Blackpool store, 1960s.

In the 1950s, Marks & Spencer intended to offset the dislocation caused by the Second World War and its aftermath by initiating a radical reconstruction programme of store development. The 1960s witnessed a large increase in the company's turnover, especially in the sales of textiles (*St Michael News*, May 1967: 1). By the end of the decade, the company had a total selling space of over 371,612 sq. metres (4 million sq. ft) located in 245 'modern stores' (*St Michael News*, Autumn 1969: 4).

Many of the design innovations in the immediate post-war period were in womenswear, especially outerwear, reflecting the needs of a market hungry for new fashions and glamour after the deprivations of the war. For menswear, meanwhile, the real breakthrough came in 1972 with the establishment of the men's suits department. The examples considered in this chapter represent a small selection of the clothing ranges sold by Marks & Spencer but it is useful here to highlight those that illustrate the ways in which Marks & Spencer was looking directly to the designer end of fashion generally and to Parisian couture in particular, translating high fashion into its own merchandise and bringing it to its very diverse and broad customer base.

One of the most successful ranges for Marks & Spencer in the 1950s was in jersey-wear (Fig. 17), the company claiming that the inspiration had come from the Paris couture collections (*St Michael News*, July 1953: 1). In 1953, wool jersey garments were available in dresses, cardigans, blouses and skirts. The idea was that these garments could be interchanged and coordinated with each other and, significantly, the double jersey fabric used was one of the first fabrics for which colour standardization (see Chapter 2) was established in the early 1950s, facilitating colour matching and the concept of jersey 'mates'. The success of Marks & Spencer jerseywear illustrates the interdependence between developments in technology and changing perceptions of fashion. Colours for these ranges were either 'classic' (various shades of grey) or 'fashionable' (cherry, emerald, gold and purple) and included 'fashion-right graphite' and lime green.

These clothes must have been extremely useful for women who needed to be smart as well as comfortable and who could afford only a modest wardrobe in which a few, well-chosen pieces could be variously coordinated with each other. For example, twin-sets could be coordinated with either pencil, flared or pleated skirts. Contrast edgings were sometimes added for interest, as were new fabrics – for example, jersey 'tweeds' (ibid.) and, in 1955, bouclé cloth, which was announced as the latest 'fashion' fabric (*St Michael News*, 18 March 1955: 5). Accessorized with buttons, belts and buckles 'in line with current fashion thought on the Continent', French *Vogue* featured one of the lines in 1953 (*St Michael News*, July 1953: 1–2). In 1954, a special edition of *St Michael News* 'brought home the jersey story in glorious technicolour' (*St Michael News*, 'Jerseywear Special', August 1954: 1). While black was clearly a favourite colour, apricot, tangerine, jungle green and jade were the fashion colours for the season, and the jersey dress had become 'an all-the-year-round fashion garment' (ibid.).

Surviving correspondence at the Marks & Spencer Archive confirms that the Paris-based designer Anny Blatt (of 27, Boulevard Malesherbes) worked on the jerseywear and knitwear ranges in a consultancy capacity for much of the 1950s, and was at least partly responsible for injecting these ranges with a fashion 'edge'.[5] A well-known designer in her own right (Interview with Ismar Glasman, 20 January 1997), Anny Blatt was initially employed by Marks & Spencer for a year: her remit was to come over from Paris once a month in order, wrote Marcus Sieff, 'to go through our ranges and to advise us accordingly':

> Special attention will be paid to our Export Knitwear … In addition, it is proposed that a small office shall be set up in Anny Blatt's establishment – not under our name. The personnel for this office will be paid for by us, and it is proposed to collect ideas and goods which will be utilized both in the home market and for export. (M. Sieff to B. Goodman, 17 October 1951, Marks & Spencer Archive)

Invoices from the early 1950s reveal that Anny Blatt's input must have been significant during this period. In June 1952, she was paid a total of £3,000[6] and although it is difficult to know how many visits this covered, it is likely that this was the total reimbursement from the time of her initial employment, in the autumn of the previous year, to this date. This covered her consultant's fees alone. Expenses were on top, as was the money paid for 'models supplied by Madame Anny Blatt'. The latter were, presumably, used as inspiration for the design, fabric and colour of the Marks & Spencer ranges. In the period October 1951 to 16 February 1954, models supplied to Marks & Spencer totalled hundreds in number (Anon., 19 February 1954, Marks & Spencer Archive). Each of Anny Blatt's visits lasted approximately five days and consisted of 'examining, criticizing and advising on styling, colouring and materials' (ibid.). Further correspondence some years later (1957) proposes that Anny Blatt should visit Marks & Spencer four to six times a year to give advice on 'the forward fashions in jersey and knitwear and also on forward colour and fabric trends'. She was to be paid £200[7] per visit (B. Goodman to Midland Bank, 11 July 1957, Marks & Spencer Archive). Her influence on the women's ranges in the 1950s appears to have been considerable.

Aside from jerseywear, another success story of the mid-1950s was the Marspun range (Fig. 20). First available at Marks & Spencer in the 1940s and used extensively in the dress ranges, Marspun became increasingly important in the early 1950s. Marspun was a spun rayon fabric with easy-care qualities (produced by Combined

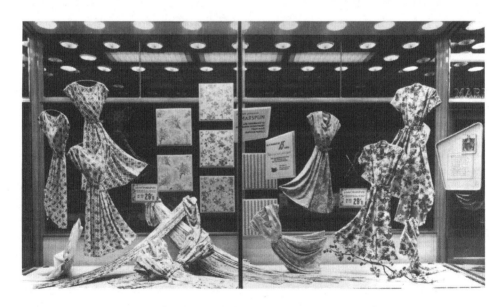

20: Window display of St Michael Marspun dresses, Coventry store, 1954.

Egyptian Mills, later known as Combined English Mills), which was exclusive to Marks & Spencer. New ideas for this vast range – there were about 3,000 different Marspun dresses by 1955 ('some 340 Paris designs and 2,000 different colour combinations') – came, as an article in *St Michael News* reported, from books, museums, from watching general trends in the fashion world including haute couture and, not least, from an analysis of the previous year's sales (*St Michael News*, 17 December 1954: 1–2). In terms of styling, Christian Dior's 'New Look' with its emphasis on longer, fuller skirts with a nipped-in waist, provided the inspiration for much of the world of fashion during the 1950s, and the influence of Dior is apparent in dress styles available at Marks & Spencer at this time. For example, *the* look for summer 1956 constituted a full cotton skirt (cut from a full circle of fabric, with a 5.5-m/6-yd hem), worn with a twinset and coloured nylon gloves.

In addition, there were significant advances made in the underwear and hosiery ranges. The company noted 'increased interest' in corsetry after the war (*St Michael News*, November 1953:1), reflecting the pervasive influence of the New Look at all levels of the market. There were two main types sold by Marks & Spencer at this time: elasticated 'roll-ons' and more rigid corsets. The latter fastened down the side with hooks and eyes. (In the 1960s, corsets were replaced by 'girdles' for which the new 'wonder fabric' Lycra was first utilized by the company in 1961) (*St Michael News*, December 1961: 3). Stockings and suspenders were worn with corsets and subsequently girdles. In 1957, the company announced developments in seam-free stockings (sold at 6s 11d^8), as well as fully fashioned 'superfit tailored' nylons, which would not wrinkle around the ankle, nor would the seams 'ride round' (*St Michael News*, September 1957: 1). A few years later, seam-free 'micromesh' stockings were selling well, with 'American tan' 'again forecast to be the best-selling colour' for summer 1963 (*St Michael News*, February 1963: 3).

By the end of the 1950s, skirt lengths were becoming shorter. This trend was mirrored at Marks & Spencer when, in 1958, the company altered all its skirt contracts to make two lengths, 71 cm (28 in) and 76 cm (30 in), instead of 73.5 cm (29 in) and 78.5 cm (31 in) (*St Michael News*, March 1958: 1). 'Women', explained Marks & Spencer's fashion commentator Mary Welbeck, 'are beginning to reveal inches of leg that haven't seen public admiration since before the New Look' (ibid.: 4). In 1966, skirts continued to get shorter, but they were clearly not short enough for some tastes. In the autumn, the *Daily Mirror* was advocating St Michael kilts for 10-year-olds to be worn as mini-kilts by 21-year-olds (*St Michael News*, November 1966: 2). In fact, Vicky Hodge, a model who was 1.75 m (5 ft 9 in) tall, apparently wore a Marks & Spencer mini-kilt designed for children aged three to four (*St Michael News*, April 1972: 1). It is significant that some of the clothing available from Marks & Spencer that hit fashion headlines at this time was fashionable because of the fact that it was worn in a different way to that intended, and by a customer who was not the one it was aimed at. Shorter hemlines – the shortest length of Marks &

Spencer's women's (as opposed to girls') skirts in the 1960s was 45.5 cm (18 in) in 1968 – contributed to successful trials of tights in the company's top stores. Described by Marks & Spencer as 'the best and only way to bridge the mini-gap', the popularity of tights thus reflected changing fashions in skirt lengths, but, interestingly, they remained fashionable even when skirts became longer once again in the 1970s (when the ratio of sales of tights to stockings at Marks & Spencer was about 80 per cent to 20 per cent) (*St Michael News*, August 1971: 6).

In the mid-1960s, the head of the design department, Hans Schneider, sought inspiration from well-known designers. He acknowledged the influence of Balenciaga as 'the leader in the great classic tradition', while describing Yves Saint-Laurent as the leader of the 'boutique trends' (*St Michael News*, January 1967: 2). Schneider's reverential reference to Balenciaga is especially noteworthy, particularly in the light of the fact that in 1962 Marks & Spencer had appointed the couturier Michael of Carlos Place (known as 'Mr Michael' to the Marks & Spencer in-house designers) to work for the company as a consultant (Rees 1973: 217). Born Michael Donéllan in Ireland in 1931, he spent several years with Lachasse before opening his own couture house in 1953. As Amy de la Haye observes, Michael was renowned for his 'stylish tailoring and strong, uncluttered design statements' and his work was often likened to that of Balenciaga (de la Haye 1996: 206). Schneider's admiration for Balenciaga's work may thus help to account for Michael's appointment.

The employment of consultants by clothing retailers was not, however, unique to Marks & Spencer on the 1960s high street. For example, Katrina Honeyman notes that Hepworth – which by 1914 had become the largest manufacturer and distributor of men's clothing (overtaken only by Burton's in the inter-war years (Honeyman 2000: 65), and from the 1950s faced with competition from Marks & Spencer and Littlewoods (ibid.: 98) – used design consultants from early on in the decade. Hardy Amies was employed by Hepworth from 1961 and Pierre Cardin by Associated Tailors, although Honeyman argues that the impact that these designers would have had was probably insufficiently radical and that in any case, business multiples such as these, 'which were built on a single standard product [the male suit] were poorly equipped to produce the variety of garments that came to comprise the male wardrobe' (ibid.: 104).

On the other hand, it is enlightening to read accounts, written in the 1950s, of fabrics and styles at Marks & Spencer that would hardly be considered fashionable today, but which clearly were at the time they were introduced. Susannah Handley observes how nylon, polyester and acrylic, for example (discussed in Chapter 2), 'were ultimately the fibres that delivered high fashion to the high street' and that Marks & Spencer was instrumental in this process (Handley 1999: 69–70). Ismar Glasman comments that although at first these new fabrics did not have a high aesthetic value, they produced 'popular fashion' with high-performance qualities (Interview with Ismar Glasman, 20 January 1997). The introduction of nylon into

Marks & Spencer lingerie (in about 1950) was considered particularly newsworthy (Fig. 10). A reporter for *St Michael News* in 1953 describes how 'one of London's most exclusive couturiers' (no name is given) praises the contribution of Marks & Spencer to fashion: 'Your policy of combining the best popular taste with the best materials at reasonable prices, has meant that every woman in England can have at least some top-quality nylon in her wardrobe' (*St Michael News*, October 1953: 3). Nylon's easy-care, drip-dry qualities and its versatility made it extremely popular. A huge variety of nylon, in different thicknesses and textures, followed for use in blouses and lingerie: permanently pleated nylon (1955), nylon crêpe de Chine, nylon seersucker and 'ninon' nylon (very sheer and transparent). By the end of the decade, matching sets of nylon lingerie could be purchased in a variety of colours: flame, blue, pink, aqua and yellow (*St Michael News*, March 1958: 1). Lingerie was for a long time considered one of the most fashion-conscious areas of the business: in 1956, Marks & Spencer followed a policy of continuous upgrading of the design of St Michael bras, which involved closer collaboration between the design and bra departments and suppliers (*St Michael News*, 3 August 1956: 2). In the 1950s, Marks & Spencer had a 15 per cent market share for bras alone (Anon. 1953, *Fashions and Fabrics*: 9, Marks & Spencer Archive) which, by the mid-1990s, had grown to an estimated 39 per cent of the total bra market (*Drapers Record*, 22 February 1997: 4). The company proudly reported that: 'Many of London's most glamorous and successful models buy their lingerie from our stores.' Vibrant colours for lingerie were the key to sales appeal: for example, women's pyjamas were sold in lilac, gold, champagne and pale green. Nightdresses, meanwhile, were available in 'exotic' colours: cyclamen, violet, turquoise and shocking pink (*St Michael News*, October 1953: 3).

Hats, still an important accessory for the majority of women in the 1950s, were integral to a smart and 'respectable' appearance, providing a relatively cheap means of making a dull, outdated outfit look new and therefore enabling women on modest incomes to maintain a fashionable appearance. Indeed, Marks & Spencer prided itself on the fact that hats could be bought from their store in designs which took their inspiration from 'top-ranking Paris houses' (*St Michael News*, 'Spring Hats Special' January 1954: 2). New colour ranges such as the one for felt hats available in 1953 (fiesta, pink romance, moonlight, banana and Windsor blue) were intended to brighten up a tired outfit (*St Michael News*, 'Autumn Hats Special', August 1953: 1–2; Fig. 21). Other accessory lines, for example a 'cheerfully chequered' duffle bag, became popular as a fashion item among the young, rather like the small backpack in the mid-1990s (*St Michael News*, November 1958: 2).

By the early 1960s, beachwear and swimwear were making fashion news. Two-piece 'bikini-style' swimsuits were being snapped up at the Marble Arch store, with 'Riviera-style' gingham ones being particularly successful (*St Michael News*, June 1960: 1); while in 1969, a best-selling towelling bikini was selling so well (over 100,000 garments sold in that year) that it was available in ten colours (*St Michael News*, July/August 1969: 3).

St Michael News

AUTUMN
HATS
SPECIAL

No. 5   MARKS & SPENCER LTD.   AUGUST, 1953

NEW *Fiesta · Banana · Moonlight*
COLOURS PAINT THE MILLINERY PICTURE

THIS autumn, the millinery picture is painted in glowing colours. In the felt range names like Fiesta, Pink Romance, Moonlight, Banana and Windsor Blue have been added to the popular but more prosaic basic colours—black, chocolate, navy and grey.

With shade cards in the stores to support the broadening of the colour range, the department is confident that the new shades will become most popular when it is seen how they can provide a colour contrast for outfits in the basic shades.

High-fashion half-hats at 15/11d. and an exciting new brushed-wool swansdown white at 12/6d. are two of the main items in what promises to be one of the Company's best millinery seasons, now that the counters in every store have virtually been "cleared for action" for autumn trading.

As in previous years the 15/11d. felt range has been compiled to cater for all ages. Trimmings will be varied and velvet will be extensively used, but neatness is the keynote.

The demand for soft feather mounts is consistent and this type of trimming will be widely used on hats designed for the older woman.

When it comes to display, successfully contrasted schemes can be achieved by high-lighting blocks of the basic colours with one or two of the new shades. Some suggested contrasts are: BLACK with FIESTA, or PINK ROMANCE, or CARDINAL RED, or BANANA; CHOC with MOONLIGHT or BANANA and SPARROW; NAVY with PINK ROMANCE or CARDINAL RED; GREY with MOONLIGHT or FIESTA or PINK ROMANCE.

And a very exciting effect can be given by a special of PURPLE with WINDSOR BLUE and Pink. Try it. When displays have been made up from this colour scheme a vivid and sales-compelling result has been achieved.

But the success of a scheme depends on the judgment of the person on the spot. The possibilities are endless and stores should try out their own ideas in this field, remembering always the value of giving a *new look* to the counter each week.

Headliners

Millinery looks forward to an exciting future. For, with some styles still experimental, potential high-lights on the millinery counters include such fashion-making numbers as a black velvet pill-box decorated with white Swiss guipure lace; top-of-the-fashion bill feather hats in several styles; and half-hats of ruched velvet. And, later in the season, there will be jersey hats which fit the head snugly. Some styles are shown below.

Velvet half-hats trimmed with feather pads.

An attractively-styled half-hat in ruched velvet.

Curled goose-feathers make an arresting decoration.

Velvet pill-box trimmed with Swiss guipure lace.

21: 'Autumn Hats Special', *St Michael News*, August 1953.

Marks & Spencer also began to work with fashion departments in colleges, enlisting, for example, the creativity of the fashion students of Kingston College of Art by selecting the best of their swimwear designs to be made up by the students using fabrics supplied by Marks & Spencer (*St Michael News*, Autumn 1969: 3).

The inspiration offered by designers may reflect a direct and more general response to the comparatively dowdy image of the large retail outlets in the eyes of a young 'swinging' teenager, for whom the boutiques such as Mary Quant's Bazaar (from the mid-1950s), Barbara Hulanicki's Biba and Miss Selfridge (from the mid-1960s) held a much stronger appeal. Although Marks & Spencer realized the potential of this sector of the market, as illustrated by the launch of new ranges such as the 'Young Look' in 1967 (significantly modelled by Twiggy – see Chapter 4) (Fig. 14), the 'Young St Michael' range in 1970, and the 'Miss Michelle' range in 1979, none of these were very successful. The phenomenon of girls in the age range of eleven to fourteen buying Marks & Spencer children's kilts (the Bootle store apparently sold a whole season's stock in one week) in 1979, or that of men's oversized cardigans being worn by teenage girls as featured in the magazine *Just Seventeen* in 1989 (25 October) not only reflect the eclectic nature of British youth fashion, but also the fact that the ranges Marks & Spencer aimed specifically at this market were simply not fashion-able enough. Perhaps even more telling is the Marks & Spencer sales assistant's comments (*St Michael News*, July 1979: 3) that the teenage girls flocking to buy Marks & Spencer children's kilts were not 'the usual Marks & Spencer type of customer' but were 'more like punks really'!

THE 1970S AND 1980S: MARKS & SPENCER GOES 'UPMARKET'?

In 1976, on the retirement of Hans Schneider, Brian Godbold took over the leader-ship of the design department. Educated at Walthamstow School of Art (then headed by the legendary Daphne Brooker, who went on to become head of fashion at what would later become Kingston University) and later the Royal College of Art, Godbold brought a number of changes to the role of design at Marks & Spencer (Godbold 2000: 108–10 and 115–17). Perhaps the most significant objective on his succession to Schneider's position was the 'reform' of the department and the raising of 'the level of design competence'. Godbold explains:

> In this, thankfully, I had the support of the board of directors, which was at the time telling the suppliers to improve their own design facilities in order to improve their products and meet our quality standards. The design group's method of working would inevitably have to change if this was to happen; we became less concerned with designing in detail on behalf of the suppliers, and more concerned with fashion prediction, colour and product coordination. The move to a more strategic role for design meant the building of a more concen-trated team of high-calibre designers. (ibid.: 109)

Godbold recalls how, in 1985, Peter Salsbury, later chief executive, recommended a greater concentration on research and development, separating pattern technology from design and moving it to the technical executive (ibid.). Thus, one of the striking developments during this period was the shifting of the actual designing of garments from the design department to Marks & Spencer's suppliers, and the consequent change in the former's role to a largely advisory, consultancy and coordinating capacity for all the separate buying departments. In 1986, each area of the design group (as it was now called) – ladieswear, childrenswear, menswear and lingerie – produced a seasonal design brief (see below). This became the buying departments' 'bible' by giving 'direction to the suppliers, covering colour, fabric, print pattern and styling' (ibid.).

Meanwhile, Marks & Spencer continued to follow the major fashion trends: in the 1970s women's skirts became longer once more and flared trousers for both women (Fig. 22) and men were popular. The company even picked up on short-lived

LEFT:
Courtelle bouclé
pants suit £7.50.
White rayon scarf
45p.
White vinyl
sandals £1.75.
BELOW:
Courtelle
nylon bouclé
jumper £1.99.
Cotton corduroy
jeans in cream
£2.99. Sling-back
vinyl flatties
£1.10.

22: Green Courtelle flared trouser suit, *St Michael News*, Spring/Summer 1971.

fashions, such as the ra-ra skirt (a short, tiered skirt) in 1982 (*St Michael News*, May 1982: 1). The challenge was to customize the more extreme trends by selling more commercial versions, in effect tempering the aesthetic ideal with the reality of mass production – and mass consumption, of course. At this time, the role of Marks & Spencer – as that of most retailers – was to pick up on fashion trends rather than to instigate them, thus making them palatable to the customer who wanted to be fashionable without having to conform to the 'excesses' or expense of high fashion. Arguably, the result was that the company marketed watered-down versions that were then less attractive precisely because they lacked the flair of the original.

Synthetic fabrics were still considered fashionable in the early 1970s, but natural fabrics came into their own once more. In particular, fabrics such as denim and cheesecloth were available at Marks & Spencer, reflecting clothing trends made popular by the hippy movement (*St Michael News*, April 1977: 3). Having competed with the acrylics (Acrilan, Orlon and Courtelle) for twenty years, wool became important again at this time, not only for knitwear but also for woven fabrics for suits. Innovations such as 'Cool Wool', promoted by Marks & Spencer in conjunction with the International Wool Secretariat (IWS), helped to add prestige to the men's and women's suit ranges from the late 1980s and did much to reinvent the traditional, staid image hitherto associated with wool (*St Michael News*, March 1986: 3).

The introduction of suits into the menswear ranges in the early 1970s marked a significant development in terms of the company's efforts to give men's clothing a more fashionable image (Briggs 1984: 60). Marcus Sieff recalls that although the manufacture of suits at this time had virtually ceased in Britain, Activon (a subsidiary of the Daks-Simpson group) began to manufacture for Marks & Spencer in 1972. Dewhirst, Marks & Spencer's longest-standing supplier (see Chapter 1), began to supply suits to the company shortly after. The success of the retailing of men's suits by Marks & Spencer was, in part, due to the employment of Italian designer Angelo Vittucci as a consultant to the menswear group from 1970 (M. Sieff 1988: 275–6).

Luxury fabrics were also introduced. In 1974, men's cashmere sweaters and women's cashmere jumpers and cardigans were trialled in small quantities at selected stores (*St Michael News*, July 1974: 3). A decade later, trials of women's coordinated silk separates and suede and leather garments were under way (*St Michael News*, September 1984: 1 and 7). Linen was also introduced into men's jackets (*St Michael News*, April 1986: 5). The development of higher-priced 'luxury' merchandise gave rise to a number of comments in the fashion press that Marks & Spencer was going 'upmarket'. For journalist Barbara Griggs, the evidence for this apparent trend was to be found in the appearance of cashmere sweaters selling for £21[9] in selected stores. In an article written for the *Daily Mail*, tellingly entitled 'I Wonder ... Could Marks & Spencer for Once Be Slipping Up?', Griggs announced that Marks & Spencer was becoming 'plummier'. She was critical of the fact that 'the fashion plums' (which, she conceded, had always been available at Marks & Spencer) 'are getting pricier' (*Daily Mail*, 13 December 1976:12).

As if in belated confirmation of this trend, an eight-page promotion of Marks & Spencer coats appeared in the September 1986 issue of *Vogue*. Reactions to what seemed to be happening at Marks & Spencer were ambivalent. While some newspapers applauded the company for responding quickly to criticism of its 'dowdy image' and facing up to competition from new high-street chains such as Next, there was also (as reflected in Griggs's article for the *Daily Mail* cited above) implied criticism that Marks & Spencer was 'abandoning' its traditional customer. However, Clinton Silver, then director responsible for clothing, countered the 'accusation' by pointing out that the opening of the extension at the flagship Marble Arch, London store in 1987 brought in journalists whose gaze slid past the usual ranges of low- and mid-priced goods to alight on the far smaller numbers of high-priced lines. Far from introducing expensive ranges, Silver argued, Marks & Spencer had always had a 'tiered catalogue', with St Michael goods located in three main price ranges – describing these as 'easy, mid and upper' (quoted in Urry, *Financial Times*, 21 May 1988). Part of the initial success of companies such as Next (established in 1982 by George Davies as an offshoot of the former menswear multiple, Hepworth) was the way in which the company targeted a defined customer, initially 'smart, better-off women in the twenty-five to thirty-five age band' (Mort 1996: 122). Marks & Spencer, on the other hand, had built its initial success on selling good-quality and well-designed garments to low-income customers (in a very much broader age range), who had previously been unable to exercise a great deal of choice in what they could buy off the peg. As we have seen, as the company grew, it began to cater for a larger proportion of the population, what Silver described as a 'tiered catalogue'. But this very broad customer base was perhaps becoming increasingly unwieldy and, along with changing market conditions, seemed to be turning off some of Marks & Spencer's customers.

Marks & Spencer's policy during the early 1980s was to buy from British suppliers where possible, but by the end of the decade, intensifying competition on the British high street and recognition of the relentless trend towards the internationalization of the fashion business – both in terms of the manufacturing base and in terms of the demand for, and consumption of, clothing – brought about a reappraisal of this policy. By the middle of the decade, Marks & Spencer was increasingly looking abroad to specific areas of excellence in order to 'upgrade' its clothing ranges (see Chapter 5). For example, the Italian leather and knitwear industries were held up as examples of excellence in manufacture and design. For men's suits, Italy also became the paradigm for fabric quality and sophisticated design. This trend continued into the 1990s.

One of a number of in-house 'scrutinies' initiated by Derek (Lord) Rayner (chairman 1984–91) resulted in a commitment by the company to concentrate on the development of staple and more classic ranges and to avoid having too many styles and no stock in depth (*St Michael News*, August 1985: 4). As part of Marks & Spencer's reappraisal of its image from the design perspective, the late 1980s also saw the company's enlistment of a new generation of independent, high-profile designers to work for Marks & Spencer in a consultancy capacity. For example, in 1985 menswear designer Paul Smith was appointed as a consultant (Godbold 2000: 109). Bruce Oldfield's appointment, at the end of 1987, gave Marks & Spencer considerable prestige not least because of the fact that Oldfield already designed clothes for members of the Royal Family, including Princess Diana, and well-known actresses. In 1990, Betty Jackson (winner of the British Fashion Council's Designer of the Year Award in 1985) was employed as a consultant for ladieswear, helping Marks & Spencer to 'create classic ranges with a sharp fashion edge' (*The M&S Magazine*, Summer 1995: 44–5). As Marks & Spencer explained, these consultants were not employed to *design* for Marks & Spencer, but their role was to act as 'constructive critics several times a year when the in-house team has put together its designs for the coming season … They help to edit and advise on everything from colour to cloth, suggesting changes where necessary' (*The M&S Magazine*, Spring 1988: 78).

Thus designers began to play a key role in bridging the gap between the world of high fashion and that of the high street, either as consultants or, later in the 1990s, as designers of specific clothing ranges to be sold by the major clothing retail chains (see below). Ironically, although Marks & Spencer played an important role in realizing this initiative, the credit is rarely attributed to the company, probably largely due to the fact that it did little overtly to promote either itself or the designers with whom it was working.[10]

THE DESIGN BRIEF

As we have seen, by the mid-1980s, the activities of the design department (design group, as it was now called) had shifted from designing and pattern-cutting to adopting more of an interpretative role. The design brief was first introduced in 1986 to represent the design department's assimilation of all the major fashion trends for a particular season and to act as a design guide for the whole Marks & Spencer clothing business. Initially, it was produced twice a year (autumn/winter and spring/summer). A number of dominant fashion 'themes' or 'moods' would be selected from the major trade and fabric or yarn fairs, including Première Vision, and the advice of fashion prediction agencies enlisted. For each of the themes, overviews of colour, fabric, pattern and product were developed by the design group, which then became the company's blueprint for that season's buying strategies for the entire Marks & Spencer clothing business.

The purpose of the design brief was to ensure coordination in terms of colour, print and styling of clothing throughout the company, vital for a business of the size

Marks & Spencer had become by this time. For example, in order for colour coordination to be achieved, the colour palette had to be kept relatively limited because too many colours would be unmanageable across all the Marks & Spencer buying departments (*Draper's Record*, 23 May 1987). Selectors and merchandisers translated the design brief into an appropriate buying strategy for individual product areas. Working closely with selectors, the designers employed by Marks & Spencer's suppliers then had to begin the task of creating the 'prototype' garments and the basis of the Marks & Spencer clothing ranges. Soon after the introduction of the design brief, a computer-aided design (CAD) system was introduced. This had the potential to transform the way Marks & Spencer and suppliers would plan clothing ranges (*St Michael News*, January 1987: 9).

THE 1990S

While high-street retailers in the 1970s and 1980s essentially followed, rather than instigated, fashion trends, a new phenomenon seemed to be emerging in the 1990s. For example, fashion writer Marion Hume observed that in Britain 'the high street is ahead of designers', with retailers such as Marks & Spencer having become more 'fashion forward' (Hume, *The Independent*, 2 December 1994: 21). Certainly the high profile enjoyed by Marks & Spencer in the fashion press appeared to confirm this and the design centre (as it was now called) took the Marks & Spencer clothing product from strength to strength. Much of the success of the company's clothing business continued to focus on selling classic lines. It is significant that in 1994 and 1995, Marks & Spencer won the British Fashion Council's award for classic design. Increasingly, however, these classic ranges were consciously injected with a strong fashion element. A good example of this was a best-selling women's double-breasted blazer in pure wool, inspired by the version sold originally at Marks & Spencer's Brooks Brothers stores in the USA (Fig. 23). The men's polo shirt sold at Marks & Spencer from the late 1980s may be described as another 'design classic'. In a review of twenty-two different makes of polo shirt undertaken by the magazine *Options* in 1989, the Marks & Spencer version (available in twenty-two colours) came out top, alongside those retailed by Blazer and John Smedley (which, however, were more expensive). The Marks & Spencer product was therefore selected as the best value for money (*Options*, Summer 1989: 55). Classic luxury garments, such as a 'relatively low-priced' Marks & Spencer grey cashmere jumper (£80) and matching cardigan (£99), were praised by Grace Bradberry in *The Times* (Bradberry, *The Times*, 16 November 1996: 3). The same crew-neck jumper appeared in *The Guardian's* regular Wednesday fashion column, 'Cheat Chic', costing 'next to nothing' when compared with 'the real thing' from N. Peal in London's Burlington Arcade, the latter costing £160 (*The Guardian*, 8 January 1997, tabloid: 10).

Furthermore, a number of Marks & Spencer products – such as the lingerie ranges – were able to compete in design terms with more exclusive labels such as La Perla,

Blazing a trail. Blazer, as before; lambswool polo-neck, £19.99; navy leggings, £15.99; loafers, £29.95. All from a selection at M&S stores. For further details turn to page 96. Hair: Thomas Dunkin at Marina Jones. Make-up: Kim Crocker at Marina Jones. Jewellery: Cobra & Bellamy, Angie Gooderham

PHOTOGRAPHS:
MARTYN THOMPSON

23: Double-breasted blazer and leggings, *The M&S Magazine*, Autumn 1991.

but cost a fraction of the price to purchase. The trend towards glamorous and fash-ionable lingerie had begun in the 1980s with an emphasis on both colour and fabrics, with satins, lace and embroidery selling well (*St Michael News*, June 1983: 5–7), while even the ranges of thermal underwear were injected with a 'fashion edge' (*St Michael News*, November 1984: 10). The idea of collections of lingerie such as 'Feathers' in 1985 and the 'Rose Collection' in 1986 were designed to appeal to the customer's desire to collect a whole range (*St Michael News*, September 1985: 5). The 'Fortuny Pleat' range (Fig. 24) (consciously named after the designer) in 1991 confirmed the high-fashion, glamorous image fast becoming associated with Marks

Finely pleated satin combined with stretch lace for luxury and comfort.
Lacy underwired bra, £14.99, and briefs with lace inset, £5.99 (above).
Styled teddy with lace top and sleeves, £25 (top left). Black lacy bustier,
£19.99, with French knickers, £12.99 (below left). Chemise teddy, £25
(below). All from a selection at M&S. For further details, turn
to page 104. Hair and make-up: Laurence Close at Camilla Arthur

PHOTOGRAPHS: SARA WILSON

24: 'Fortuny Pleat' range of underwear, *The M&S Magazine*, Winter 1991.

& Spencer lingerie (Ewing 1993: 274). The 'worn to be seen' range in the early 1990s
and the introduction of the bodysuit (or 'body', as it popularly came to be known)
reflected the wider vogue for underwear being worn as outerwear and the popularity
of Lycra.

It would not be an exaggeration to say that the success of the lingerie and hosiery
ranges at this period was in no small part due to the inclusion of Lycra in Marks &
Spencer's core ranges. In 1988, Marks & Spencer had announced the launch of a new
range of hosiery with Lycra (Fig. 25). This was just the start of the success Lycra

25: Lycra hosiery, *The M&S Magazine*, Autumn/Winter 1988.

would have in making possible comfortable, more casual dressing, perhaps epitomized by the ubiquitous Lycra leggings in the late 1980s and into the 1990s (Fig. 23). To what extent the move towards more casual dressing in the 1990s can be attributed to the phenomenal success and versatility of Lycra, it is difficult to say, but by the mid-1990s, observes Handley, 'leggings were a mainstay in the wardrobe of all ages and all sizes and have been one of Marks & Spencer's greatest success stories' along with thousands of Lycra bodies (Handley 1999: 150). As Handley points out, 'When it comes to fashion prestige, the fact that a Lycra swing ticket hangs from an

Armani jacket adds reflected value to every Marks & Spencer garment with the same logo' (ibid.).

In menswear, Italian expertise was enlisted for the new 'Italian Collections' in the early 1990s. This was part of a major overhaul of men's suits, in which Marks & Spencer technologists and selectors worked closely with both the company's Italian and British manufacturers on design and tailoring (*The M&S Magazine*, Winter 1990: 60–1). A number of the fabrics used for Marks & Spencer suits were sourced from leading Italian manufacturer, Marzotto, a supplier for Giorgio Armani (Tredre, *The Independent*, 22 September 1990: 32). Indeed, an article in *The Economist* in 1998 describes how, at the Marzotto warehouse, 'a row of Gianfranco Ferre suits hang alongside a row of equally smart, albeit less flashy, blazers destined for Marks & Spencer' (*The Economist*, 11 April 1998: 65).

Alongside these developments, the fashion press took a new interest in Marks & Spencer. A series of articles focused upon the company's supposed 'reinvention' of its image. For example, Sally Brampton observed, in an article appositely entitled 'The Adoration of St Michael', how 'really fashionable women' had begun to shop at Marks & Spencer (Brampton, *Guardian Weekend*, 8 October 1994: 40–44 and 56). In the April 1995 edition of *Vogue*, Mimi Spencer referred to Marks & Spencer's 'sartorial conversion', declaring that:

> The company that once specialized in populist fashion of the lowest common denominator – drip-dry skirts with elasticated waists and the knickers of a nation – is on the fashion offensive. St Michael, revered as the patron saint of basics for a century, is now blessing us with not-quite-Joseph angora knits, near-Prada peacoats and hint-of-Hindmarch bags. (Spencer, *Vogue*, April 1995: 26)

As if in confirmation of Marks & Spencer's newfound status among the gurus of high fashion, the supermodel Amber Valetta appeared on the front cover of *Vogue* in May 1996 wearing a £21 Marks & Spencer polyester shantung shirt. The company had apparently thrown off its working-class roots along with its populist appeal, and started to concentrate its market potential on a more 'discerning' customer.

The problem with this interpretation is that it fails to appreciate the role the company was playing in making popular fashion available some fifty years previously. Without wishing to undervalue the innovations that took place at Marks & Spencer from the early 1990s, it is important to see these developments in their historical perspective. In the early days of the Penny Bazaars and into the 1930s, the vast majority of Marks & Spencer's customers were working class. By the end of the 1950s, however, both the Marks & Spencer product and the nature of the market had changed, as if in tandem with each other. The quest for excellence of design and product was reflected both in the drive towards the introduction of new fabrics (see Chapter 2) and, as we have seen, in the employment of design consultants. Thus, in the period after the Second World War, Marks & Spencer clothes were not only being bought by the company's 'traditional' working-class customer. They were also making a direct appeal to the middle classes, partly perhaps because after the war, Breward points out, 'a middle-class market accustomed to such standardization was far more receptive to the value and quality represented in mass-produced clothes (Breward 2003: 57).

THE ISSUE OF DESIGN ORIGINALITY

Ironically, perhaps, it was the positive press that Marks & Spencer received based on its 'new' interest in design and creating a fashionable image which, it could be argued, led to some extent to the criticism levelled at the company prior to the downturn in profits towards the end of the 1990s. Although this study does not aim to 'explain' the company's present in the light of its past, it was perhaps Marks & Spencer's reputation for being beyond reproach that then threw the company into the spotlight when accusations of design plagiarism were made in the 1990s. Judi Bevan (2002) begins her analysis in spring 1998 and makes no mention of this issue as being a contributory factor to the company's downturn in fortunes in the late 1990s. However it is probable that the controversy surrounding Liza Bruce's accusation that Marks & Spencer had copied one of her designs – as presented by ITV's *World in Action* (15 January 1996) – was potentially extremely damaging. This report made allegations that Marks & Spencer had copied, among other products, a design 'original' – a dip-dyed swimsuit by Liza Bruce. Indeed, the explicit message of the programme was that Marks & Spencer was largely to blame for the financial straits that Liza Bruce and her company found themselves in. However one-sided in its handling of the story, the report is likely to have shocked even the most loyal of Marks & Spencer's customers. It certainly raised significant issues regarding the process of design origination.

In the 1990s, there was much discussion in the media about the changing relationship between the designer and the high-street chains. For a long time, the high-street clothing chains were assumed to have been following what was seen on the catwalks, but in the late 1990s, the high street – as Marion Hume's article (Hume, *The Independent*, 2 December 1994: 21) cited above claims – appeared suddenly to lead the way in terms of establishing new trends. It is probably no coincidence that at about the same time, discussion regarding issues relating to design origination and copyright led to, for example, the establishment of ACID (Anti-Copying in Design) in 1996. ACID was formed in order to act on behalf of small firms in dispute over copyright cases. Its long-term aim was to invite retailers to join and have access to their database, so that if new products came on to the market they could check to see whether the design had been copied (Oldfield, *The Sunday Times*, 27 October 1996: 13). It is perhaps useful at this point to provide some historical background to this complex issue.

In the nineteenth century, design copyright was largely controlled by the Design Copyright Act of 1839 (Levitt 1986: 3–6). This act reflected the need to protect, by copyright, the originator of a particular design from potential plagiarism. The 1883 Patents, Designs and Trademarks Act created a new category of registered designs for 'articles of wearing apparel'. This provided formal recognition of the developing ready-to-wear industry. By the early decades of the twentieth century, however, it seems to have been generally accepted by the fashion industry as a whole that with the proliferation of ready-to-wear companies at all levels, it was becoming increasingly difficult to control the process by which designer originals could be 'interpreted'. In the 1930s, companies such as Jaeger, Cresta, Deréta and Dorville had profitable businesses producing 'models', more often than not based on Paris originals. The launch of Christian Dior's 'Corolle' line in spring 1947 – the 'New Look' as it came to be widely known – prompted wholesale imitation, not only at all levels of the ready-to-wear clothing industry, but by the home dressmaker making or altering her own clothes. Ingenuity was put to the test when women added fabric to the hems of their skirts – albeit sometimes in a different fabric from the rest of the garment – in order to make it resemble in some way a Dior original. Interestingly, this was not necessarily seen to be a threat to the profitability of the originator of the design. In fact, it may have given the original even greater prestige and exposure. In any case, the impact of the New Look continued to be felt well into the 1950s. A list of 'models' purchased by Marks & Spencer from Paris in the 1950s and imported from France under import licence exists at the Marks & Spencer Archive. Many of these samples originated from Anny Blatt (discussed earlier) but others were designed by André Ledeux, Jean Baillie and Les Couturiers Associés (Anon., 2 January 1952, Marks & Spencer Archive). Brian Godbold describes working for Wallis in the 1960s before joining Marks & Spencer, and comments on similar practices:

> One of Wallis's greatest successes was the 'Pick of Paris' range, which featured inexpensive couture copies and it fell upon me to go to Paris to select coats from the autumn 1969 collections. This was a widespread and quite legitimate design practice; we attended the shows as buyers and developed the garments we chose back in London, modifying the cut, fit and finish to suit our market and price. (Godbold 2000: 107)

The famous designer Gabrielle Chanel appeared to be unperturbed about her designs being 'interpreted', believing that those who insisted on their own originality had 'no memory' and that 'fashion does not exist until it goes down into the streets' (Charles-Roux 1982: 237). The simplicity of Chanel's designs meant that 'more or less clandestine copies' became possible (Mackrell 1992: 12). Indeed, according to her biographer Edmonde Charles-Roux, Chanel was 'a creator of original designs who was only happy when being plagiarized by others' (Charles-Roux 1989: xvii). Furthermore, it could be argued that there is little that is entirely original in contemporary fashion in terms of cut, styling or fabric. However, the intensely competitive nature of the fashion industry and concern about the precarious status of the designer in Britain – and the much debated 'designer drain' from Britain to countries which had traditionally given the fashion designer more support – gave rise to alarm at what appeared to be widespread copying by retailers of original designs. What was traditionally described as the 'trickle-down effect' (however inaccurate as a general explanation of the diffusion of fashion), seemed, in some cases, to have become a veritable waterfall. The lapse of time between the point at which styles were seen on the catwalk capitals of the world and then on the high street was contracting. This phenomenon – as well as, no doubt, the hype fed by the media's taste for a story – may help to account for the one-sided approach taken by the ITV *World in Action* programme.

The developments that took place within Marks & Spencer and the company's suppliers, from the early 1990s, to harness the expertise of designers in a variety of ways are of significance, particularly in light of the tone of ITV's *World in Action* report. Not only had designers been employed as consultants by Marks & Spencer from the 1950s, but also the trend, from the 1990s, was to employ designers to create specific ranges of clothing for the major high-street clothing retailers.

DESIGNERS FOR THE HIGH STREET

The launch of Marks & Spencer's Autograph range in spring 2000 reflected a new phase in the relationship between designers and retailers. Marks & Spencer worked directly with independent designers such as Betty Jackson, Julien MacDonald and Katherine Hamnett to produce small collections for sale in stylishly decorated, dedicated areas within top stores (Godbold 2000: 115–6). However, this trend had already begun some years earlier. In the early 1990s, Sally Smith, design director for Coats Viyella (one of the largest suppliers at this time to Marks & Spencer), wanted to involve and support designers working in Britain, and in 1994 designer Tanya Sarne (of the successful Ghost label) was asked to design a range of dresses for manufacture by Coats Viyella and retail by Marks & Spencer. The range was enormously successful and pioneered the way for designers, suppliers and retailers to work successfully together for mutual benefit. Indeed, by 1997, Coats Viyella had deals not only with Tanya Sarne (for dresses), but Marion Foale (for cardigan 'jackets') and Jeff Griffin (for menswear).

The role of suppliers in making the crucial link between design, design education and the retailing of clothing has been highly significant in other ways. In an interview (8 April 1997) with the then design director for the Dewhirst Group (then Marks & Spencer's longest-standing supplier), Michael Terry described the ways in which Dewhirst utilized its design links for specific projects, rather than using 'outside' designers on a permanent consultancy basis. The group also forged close links with the fashion design course at Kingston University and sponsored fashion students from the early 1990s, setting projects each year in order to focus students on possible key developments, not just in future fashion trends, but in shopping/retailing practices and the future role of technology in the fashion industry.

By harnessing the skills of designers indirectly, via suppliers, to create specific ranges, it is not so much that Marks & Spencer suddenly became design-conscious but that the company and its suppliers were developing new ways of pursuing design excellence. The relationship between the designer and the high street, argued Roger Tredre in *The Observer* in 1997, 'is undergoing a spectacular transformation' (Tredre, *The Observer*, 23 February 1997: 16). Other retailers followed in the wake of Marks & Spencer. For example, Dorothy Perkins employed designer duo Suzanne Clements and Ignacio Ribeiro, Debenhams employed Jasper Conran, and BHS utilized the talent of Paul Frith.

The employment of established designers by Marks & Spencer and their suppliers was not the only way in which design talent began to be harnessed. From 1994, Marks & Spencer sponsored the New Generation which, operated by the British Fashion Council, funds emergent designers to show their collections during British (London) Fashion Week. In 1996, for example, the British Fashion Council announced that Marks & Spencer would sponsor designers Antonio Berardi, Stephen Fuller and Justin Oh (Frankel, *The Guardian*, 7 August 1996: 9).

Although the developments that took place at Marks & Spencer in the 1990s are significant in their own right – principally because they helped to nurture an essentially collaborative relationship between designers and clothing retailers – such innovations need to be assessed in the context of a well-established tradition in which Marks & Spencer made the concept of good design central to changing visions of the clothing it would retail. This chapter has argued that the pursuit of design excellence can be traced back to the establishment of the design department in 1936. Similarly, in the next chapter, the company's well-publicized employment of supermodels, from the early 1990s, will be seen in the context of a long-established tradition that acknowledges the importance of marketing and promoting the Marks & Spencer product and which reaches back to 1928 and the registration of the St Michael trademark.

In 1990, Marks & Spencer employed the high-profile model Claudia Schiffer to advertise the autumn womenswear ranges, to promote the 'new' fashionable Marks & Spencer image discussed in Chapter 3. Then, in an article for *The Times* in 1997, Grace Bradberry argued that 'Patrick Demarchelier's picture of "supermodel" Linda Evangelista in thigh-length black socks, a black miniskirt and a black polo-neck came to symbolize the new Marks & Spencer' (Bradberry, *The Times*, 19 May 1997: 17). Such an interpretation reflects a view that the employment by Marks & Spencer of supermodels in the 1990s was indicative of the company's desire to present a more fashionable image to Marks & Spencer's customers, in an uncharacteristically high-profile manner. However, just as a historical perspective enables the importance of the company's emphasis on the 'design element' in the 1990s to be seen as part of a well-established tradition rather than as a radical departure from previous company policy, so does it enable a more objective view to be established with regard to an analysis of the historical development of the company's policies for advertising and promoting its clothing. By taking a retrospective view, the employment by Marks & Spencer of supermodels in the 1990s can in fact be seen as part and parcel of a coherent policy of selling clothing reaching back to at least 1928, with the registration of the St Michael trademark. In seeking to assess the various ways in which the company has marketed and promoted its clothing ranges, this chapter will consider how, from the start, Marks & Spencer utilized a variety of sales strategies, including methods of display, store layout and, later, advertising.

SELLING THE 'RIGHT' PRODUCT

Until the 1950s, Marks & Spencer eschewed overt advertising on the whole. The company's premise was that the quality of the Marks & Spencer product 'spoke' for itself and did not require further explanation. Any advertising tended to be 'reason-why advertising' – which, observes Paul Jobling (2005), emphasized the 'logical reasons – or actual benefits – to be had from purchasing a garment ... (the price of the article and where and how to buy it, cut and fit, the materials used in its construction, and ideas concerning its overall look and quality') as distinct from 'atmospheric advertising', which tended to be more 'soft sell and symbolic' (Jobling 2005: 29–30). Thus, any advertising that was initiated by the company was generally of an informative nature, giving coverage of store extensions and the launching of new, lower-price campaigns, for example (Rees 1973: 209–10). In this respect, Marks &

Spencer's advertising can be seen in the same tradition as that of its competitors such as C&A, which in 1922 was advertising the opening of its 'Festival of Fashion' at 'London's Newest Bargain Centre', 376–384 Oxford Street.[1] C&A also advertised its mail-order service, proclaiming it in the *Daily Chronicle* (25 September 1922) to be either free or one shilling.[2] It listed the garments available, such as a 'serviceable serge coat'. The company's aim of advertising itself as a 'leader of fashion economy' and of what it described as 'the height of fashion at the lowest cost' seems to have been successful, for by December, C&A reported that: 'The policy of reducing our profits to the minimum to ensure a vast turnover has proved overwhelmingly successful, so much so that we were compelled temporarily to suspend our advertising' (*Evening News*, 4 December 1922). It would appear that advertising had had a direct impact on sales and that sales could not keep pace with demand.

Just as C&A in the early days of establishing itself in Britain promoted the clothing it sold in terms of its low price and reference to fashion, so, as we have seen, Marks & Spencer concentrated on selling a quality product at a reasonable price. As Marks & Spencer personnel perceived it, the key to the sustained success of Marks & Spencer was to choose the 'right product' – in terms of its design, quality, value, availability and so on. From the very beginning, Bookbinder observes, Michael Marks 'had to win the trust of his clientele by selling items that represented value for money' (Bookbinder 1993:14). One of the many lessons brought back by Simon Marks from the USA in the 1920s was that there could be no 'blind spots'. In other words, sales of individual products must be constantly monitored and new lines trialled before a decision was made to go into production on a large scale. Unprofitable lines were withdrawn. Israel Sieff recalls in his memoirs the importance of eradicating such blind spots:

> I learned the value of counter footage, that is, that each counter had to pay wages, rent, overhead expenses and earn a profit. There could be no blind spots on the counters in so far as goods were concerned. This meant a much more exhaustive study of the goods we were selling and the needs of the public. (I. Sieff 1970: 142)

Following Simon Marks's trip to the USA in 1924, sales information was provided by the Checking List System (discussed in Chapter 1). Sixty years on, however, a much more rapid response to sales information was facilitated via electronic point of sale (EPOS). First introduced in 1984, the company planned for EPOS to be in all stores by 1992. A report in *St Michael News* in June 1985, following a two-store trial, described how EPOS would enable buying departments to respond more rapidly to sales and therefore to customer demand (*St Michael News*, June 1985: 6), although it worked on precisely the same principle and did essentially the same job (but more accurately and more quickly) as the original Checking List System. For customers, the advantage of the new system was a detailed receipt recording every item purchased. A new head office computer system (known as BDI) was introduced in 1988 and gave merchandisers direct access to sales figures, thus enabling Marks & Spencer to respond much more rapidly to sales, including the results of trial lines. Writing for the *Financial Times* in 1988, Maggie Urry highlighted the important role that EPOS could play in monitoring sales closely and responding rapidly if necessary, even if this meant switching production from a less popular line to a more popular one:

> Last year the buyers [at Marks & Spencer] decided that short skirts would be important this year. Two basic styles were selected, straight and flared, and the fabrics were bought. The buying department reckoned that 25 per cent of its skirts would be the short, straight kind and another 7 per cent the short, fuller style. When the season started, sales of the fuller style turned out at well below the estimate, while long, flowing skirts were selling better than expected. Marks & Spencer rapidly told its suppliers to switch production from the short, full style to the long, flowing one using the same fabrics. (Urry, *Financial Times*, 21 May 1988)

In the 1990s, a high level of flexibility in the production process became not only desirable, as customers demanded more change and variety within any one season, but also absolutely essential if Marks & Spencer was to compete with chains such as New Look. It was no longer acceptable to offer ranges of garments that hung about, unchanging and becoming rather tired-looking, in stores for three or four months before going on to the reduced rail; customers were offered and began to demand something new on more or less each successive visit. When Marks & Spencer launched George Davies's *Per Una* range in autumn 2001, one of the objectives was to draw customers back into the store by merchandise that was continually changing. The turnover of fashion was accelerating, fed by changing popular perceptions of fashion.

THE ST MICHAEL REGISTERED TRADEMARK

> St Michael has become a household word for millions of people. It stands not only for quality but for fine goods at inexpensive prices. (*St Michael News*, December 1958: 4)

Until the 1980s, Marks & Spencer avoided the kind of powerful – albeit subtly presented – advertising widely accepted as being essential to the success of any business in the twenty-first century. Nevertheless, from its origins as a stall at an open market, sales strategies employed by Marks & Spencer were aimed principally at promoting the idea of quality goods at reasonable prices. The earliest example of advertising by such a definition was the slogan used by Michael Marks on the market stalls and in his Penny Bazaars: 'Don't Ask the Price, It's a Penny'. This proved to be a highly effective sales strategy, which helped to make the process of shopping respectable for working-class customers (see Chapter 1). Until 1918, the penny price point also facilitated a simple price structure which the company was able to re-establish from the latter part of the 1920s with the five-shilling maximum, the latter abandoned only in 1939. However, of these early forms of advertising, that of the greatest longevity was the use of the St Michael registered trademark, established in 1928 (Fig. 6). The St Michael brand name, promoted by Marks & Spencer as being synonymous with quality and value for money, became an established part of the company's corporate identity. Not only did it attach itself to the labels of the garments themselves, but also to the in-house magazine, *St Michael News*, discussed below.

Passed in 1875, the Trademarks Act, observes Sarah Levitt, ensured that 'the registered trademark rapidly became a guarantee of authenticity suggesting exclusiveness' (Levitt 1986: 24). It was easier to obtain than a registered design because one trademark could be used to authenticate a firm's entire output for an indefinite period (ibid.). Of particular relevance to this discussion is the fact that the trademark fulfilled an important advertising function and, according to Hamish Fraser, 'the customer came to depend on the label as a guide to quality' (Fraser 1981: 146). Significantly, one of the first trademarks to be registered under the 1875 act was the St Margaret label by the company Corah, as we have seen one of Marks & Spencer's first suppliers. The label was named after the company's St Margaret Works, opened in 1865 near St Margaret's Church, Leicester. Marks & Spencer registered its own trademark – St Michael – on 5 November 1928; it soon appeared on a range of textiles, toys and other goods and, two years later, on food.

Marks & Spencer utilized both the St Margaret (those goods manufactured by Corah) and St Michael labels until after the Second World War. However (probably to avoid confusion for the customer and to consolidate the St Michael brand), from the 1950s, all Marks & Spencer clothing, irrespective of the manufacturer, was sold solely under the St Michael label (Jopp 1965: 42–3). Only in the early 1990s, with the company's increasing international expansion into areas of the globe where Marks & Spencer could not rely on a reputation built up over more than a century, did the efficacy of the St Michael brand come into question. In 1991, the company commissioned research into customer perceptions of the relative importance of the St Michael and 'Marks & Spencer' labels. The research found that, while everyone did not acknowledge the distinction between St Michael and 'Marks & Spencer', the importance of the former lay in its recognition as a familiar visual symbol, especially for clothes. A report by consultants Taylor Nelson AGB resulted in the recommendation that a new label, 'St Michael from Marks & Spencer', should be introduced in the UK, Eire, France and Belgium, not only on clothing but on 'trucks, carrier bags and substantial products'.[3]

Not long after this, however, following rumours that Marks & Spencer was to abandon its 'patron saint', the company was quick to quash any such suggestions.

Deputy chairman Keith Oates was reported as saying: 'The St Michael brand name is recognized worldwide and is an integral part of Marks & Spencer' (*Draper's Record*, 25 November 1995: 7). Although subsequently replaced simply with the words 'Marks & Spencer' to represent those clothing ranges which were the company's own brand (as distinct from the Autograph – see Chapter 3 – or *Per Una* ranges), the St Michael brand name was undoubtedly instrumental in establishing Marks & Spencer's reputation for quality over a period of seventy years and in establishing the concept of a retail giant selling exclusively own-brand merchandise.

EXCHANGE AND REFUND POLICY

The first mention of a refund policy was in 1932. A 'new' *Marks & Spencer Magazine* (only one edition appears to survive at the Marks & Spencer Archive) reads as follows: 'Marks & Spencer do not buy seconds or sub-standard articles. Satisfaction is guaranteed either by a refund of money or exchange of articles' (*Marks & Spencer Magazine*, Summer 1932: 6). Some twenty years later, Marks & Spencer reiterated this policy, stating that: 'Any customer's complaint will be met immediately by an exchange or refund, on the spot, regardless of whether the complaint appears to be justified or not', adding that 'The customer is always and completely right' (*St Michael News*, September 1953: 2).

From the point of view of the customer, if a purchase was not 'right' for any reason, an exchange or refund would be given with no questions asked. This policy, especially in the context of the 1930s, was clearly highly unusual and it was only in 2005 that the policy was revisited. In 2005, whereas the majority of clothing retailers offered a refund if goods were returned within fourteen or, more commonly, twenty-eight days of purchase, Marks & Spencer introduced a policy limiting the refund period to ninety days. Prior to that, there was, incredibly, no official time period beyond which customers could not request a refund (in theory it could be several years, provided the garment was unworn) so long as they had proof of purchase; and even if they didn't, they were normally offered an exchange in any case, usually to the value of the latest selling price of the garment. In 1995, the *Clothes Show* conducted a survey into consumers' rights, and retailers' refund policies were analysed. Not surprisingly, Marks & Spencer was singled out because the report found that: 'The company does over and above what is required by law' (*Clothes Show*, BBC One, 10 December 1995).

In the light of the fact that Marks & Spencer did not provide fitting rooms until the 1980s, the real purchasing decision would often be made in the peace of the customer's home rather than in the frenetic store environment. As Marks & Spencer pointed out in 1955, 'The fitting room is your home' (*St Michael News*, 28 October 1955: 2). Even when fitting rooms were provided in the 1980s, Marks & Spencer's exchange and refund policy remained fundamentally unchanged. Interestingly, research conducted in the mid-1980s revealed that the provision of fitting rooms had not actually impacted significantly on the number of refunds (*St Michael News*, February 1985: 3).

Altruistic motivations aside, Marks & Spencer's exchange and refund policy may also be construed as an effective sales strategy and works on providing a safety net in the context of the customer's indecision about making a purchase. To know that a refund will be given with no questions asked and no requirement to supply personal details on receipt of the refund (name, address) is, arguably, more likely to encourage a sale than a policy which makes it time-consuming or awkward in any respect to return a garment. Notwithstanding the large number of refunds given, an actual sale is consequently more likely to be made at Marks & Spencer than in a store which has a much less favourable (from the customer's point of view) exchange and refund policy.

ST MICHAEL NEWS AND THE M&S MAGAZINE

The establishment of the in-house publication *St Michael News* in 1953 (see Acknowledgements) reflected the company's desire not only to forge a strong sense of corporate identity among its employees, but specifically to increase employees' knowledge of the products sold by the company. Written by an editorial team based at Baker Street, the magazine's tone, as Keren Protheroe points out, is 'unashamedly partisan' and 'was clearly the vehicle by which the company's retailing philosophy and brand identity were commonly understood and promoted' (Protheroe 2005: 101). Published on a regular fortnightly basis from 1955, and then at varying intervals until Christmas 1990, the kind of detailed information provided by *St Michael News* was a way of 'educating' employees about new ranges, fabric developments, and so on. The references made to *St Michael News* throughout this study reflect the range and breadth of topics covered by the publication.

The intended promotional role of *St Michael News* is evident from a cartoon that appeared in the 1955 edition about a fictitious sales assistant called Sally Sayles. Sally reads *St Michael News* and then shows it to her family, the article concluding: '… And in her modest way, Sally helps to swell the number of St Michael fans' (*St Michael News*, 22 July 1955: 3). Clearly, therefore, the publication was intended for a much wider readership than the number of employees who actually received a copy. The company's success in this matter was illustrated in 1961 when Marks & Spencer reported the results of a pilot survey: 'Most copies of *St Michael News* are read by at least six people in addition to the individual salesgirl who receives it' (*St Michael News*, January 1961: 2).

In spite of the success of *St Michael News* as a promotional tool, by the mid-1960s, the need for information more directly targeted towards the Marks & Spencer customer was evident. In 1966, for example a 'St Michael Shopping Guide' (a 16-page catalogue of winter merchandise) was inserted into the 15 October edition of *Woman* magazine (*St Michael News*, October 1966: 1). It would be another twenty-one years, however, before the company launched its own magazine for customers.

Subsequent to the launch of the Marks & Spencer charge card, the first edition of *The M&S Magazine* appeared in stores in 1987, free to charge card account holders and on sale for £1[4] to other customers. Marks & Spencer was one of the first clothing retailers to launch a customer magazine, the objectives of which, according to *Drapers Record*, were as follows:

1. To develop a more personal relationship with customers and nurture loyalty;
2. To increase sales by selling across departments;
3. To act as an effective medium, over which the retailer has editorial control, to inform customers and generate enthusiasm for merchandise.

(*Draper's Record*, 5 April 1997: 12)

By 1996, *The M&S Magazine* had a circulation figure of 2.25 million and readership of 4.622 million.[5] Meanwhile, *St Michael News* retained its 'in-house' function with special French and German editions introduced in the 1990s specifically for staff working in the company's increasing number of stores in the rest of Europe. In terms of providing detailed information about the Marks & Spencer product and of promoting the company's corporate identity, *The M&S Magazine* (See Fig. 25) had by now taken over the role of *St Michael News*.

MEDIA ADVERTISING

As with the advertising of the opening of C&A stores in the 1920s, Marks & Spencer (until the 1950s) used media advertising primarily to publicize the opening of new stores in local newspapers, such as that of the Pantheon store at Oxford Circus in the 1930s. While the company commissioned some small-scale advertising in 1955 in major towns outside London – Southampton, Bristol and Glasgow, for example – the 'company's biggest advertising experiment' to date took place in 1958. Marks & Spencer took a four-page spread in the magazine *Woman*, chosen by the company because of its wide circulation – 8,124,000 women aged sixteen and over, Marks & Spencer reported proudly (*St Michael News*, May 1958: 1). 'Our intention', explained Marks & Spencer, 'is to publicize the policy of the company and the quality and value of our goods', by drawing particular attention to summer fashions, childrenswear, hosiery, lingerie, 'slumberwear' and 'fashion foundations' (ibid.). By 1970, advertisements for Marks & Spencer clothing had been extended to other magazines: not only *Woman*, but also *Woman's Own* and *Woman and Home* (*St Michael News*, October 1970: 3). Promotions of particular fabrics took the form of colour inserts in *Woman*, for example, organized to coincide with large-scale in-store Marks & Spencer promotions, such as that for Crimplene in 1972 (*St Michael News*, June 1972: 3).

A wave of advertising initiatives, from the late 1950s, reflected to some extent the necessity of giving customers information about technological advances, in particular the qualities of new synthetic fabrics (Chapter 2). Handley observes that in the market as a whole, the synthetics 'created a very visible increase in fashion advertising during the 1950s which increased public awareness of design and changing fashion silhouettes' (Handley 1999: 75). At Marks & Spencer, fabric developments were chronicled in a number of editions of *St Michael News* as well as in the national press. For example, in 1958 men's Terylene and cotton drip-dry shirts were advertised in, amongst other national newspapers, *The Sunday Times* and *The Observer*, and 'Acrilan at Marks & Spencer' received coverage in the *Daily Mail, Daily Express* and *Daily Mirror* (*St Michael News*, December 1958: 1). In 1959, Marks & Spencer embarked upon a new advertising venture in a series of seven-second television spots organized jointly with Courtaulds. These promoted the easy-care qualities of Marks & Spencer Tricel blouses, skirts, slips and nightdresses (*St Michael News*, April 1959: 1). The company also took part in other joint advertising programmes: for example, one with British Nylon Spinners for Bri-Lon and Bri-Nylon and another with the International Wool Secretariat (IWS) (*St Michael News*, July 1959: 1 and September 1959: 6). Thus the marketing of new fabrics was often best achieved through joint promotions between Marks & Spencer and the fabric manufacturer or board representing the fabric. In 1981, a highly successful press advertising campaign costing £50,000[6] was launched for a joint Marks & Spencer–Du Pont promotion of Lycra. Featuring St Michael stretch jeans and trousers, sales during the four weeks of the promotion were reported to have been almost double those of the previous four weeks (*St Michael News*, April 1981: 2 and October 1981: 3). In August 1982, Marks & Spencer merchandise made its first appearance in *Vogue*, a jointly funded promotion between Marks & Spencer and the IWS, featuring wool garments in women's outerwear (*St Michael News*, June 1982: 2). Such a venture reflected the increasingly upmarket and fashionable profile sought by Marks & Spencer, discussed in Chapter 3.

By the late 1980s, Marks & Spencer's reappraisal of its image in a period of intense competition on the high street may be illustrated by a series of corporate advertising campaigns, which began in spring 1988. In the second series (summer 1988), five different full-colour advertisements appeared in national newspapers, Sunday papers and TV supplements. They all carried the slogan, 'Have You Been to Marks & Spencer Lately?' and were clearly intended to draw in customers who might not normally associate Marks & Spencer with a fashionable image, as well as securing the loyalty of the company's more traditional clientele. These campaigns were avowedly 'aimed at changing customers' perceptions of Marks & Spencer' (*St Michael News*, September/October 1988: 5). They continued into the early 1990s, when the company also began to employ supermodels to sell its clothing ranges.

THE EMPLOYMENT OF SUPERMODELS

> The supermodels of the nineties are icons, emblems of an industrial society that is ever more accomplished in the replication and use of selling imagery. (Gross 1995: 13)

When she advertised the autumn 1990 womenswear ranges, Claudia Schiffer was not the first high-profile model to advertise Marks & Spencer clothing. Twiggy had modelled Marks & Spencer miniskirts in the 1960s for the company's 'Young Look' range (Fig. 14) in an attempt to appeal to a more youthful and fashion-conscious customer. However, the employment by Marks & Spencer of supermodels reflected a new direction embarked upon by high-street retailers in the 1990s in order to harness the unique ability of the supermodel to sell their products as well as to redefine the particular image the product carried with it. Claudia Schiffer, Linda Evangelista, Christy Turlington and Amber Valetta are just a few of the well-known names, commanding huge fees, who have been hired by Marks & Spencer since the beginning of the 1990s. For the most part, the items of clothing advertised by the supermodels were 'wearable classics', which, according to an article in the *Daily Express* 'have more in common with the Paris ready-to-wear collections than they do with chain-store ranges' (Modlinger, *Daily Express*, 20 February 1992: 29). These innovations in womenswear set the precedent for similar developments in menswear: in 1993, for example, fashion shoots of Marks & Spencer menswear by photographer Aldo Rossi featured the 'superstar' Valentino model, Eric Osland (Smith, *Evening Standard Magazine*, 29 October 1993: 14–16). Elsewhere on the high street, other retailers followed Marks & Spencer's lead, with Helena Christensen, for example, becoming the face of Hennes and then of Dorothy Perkins.

As fashion writer Tamsin Blanchard observed in *The Independent* in 1994, Linda Evangelista can make a £30 pair of trousers look like a £300 pair, adding, 'And that, indeed, is why Marks & Spencer hires her' (Blanchard, *The Independent*, 18 November 1994). If Blanchard was correct in her assumptions, and Marks & Spencer's customers now wanted to look as if they were wearing a much more expensive item of clothing than those traditionally associated with Marks & Spencer, this is surely an indication not only of the degree to which the Marks & Spencer customer had changed since the 1930s but also the fashion market as a whole. Furthermore, women who aspired to look like Linda Evangelista could now dress like her. The level of potential sales opportunities afforded by such an investment, therefore, was evident. Aside from the increased sales generated directly as a result of employing supermodels, the celebrity status of these figures ensured that media coverage was immense, putting Marks & Spencer at the centre of the fashion spotlight, which, as Catherine Ostler observed, 'would have cost thousands had they been paid-for advertisements' (Ostler, *Mail On Sunday*, 16 April 1995: 37).

FASHION SHOWS AND EXHIBITIONS

From the 1950s, Marks & Spencer staged fashion shows around the country as a way of informing both employees (the models at these fashion shows were usually Marks & Spencer sales assistants) and customers about new products, thus promoting sales and encouraging publicity for the company (Fig. 26). One such show reported by *St*

26: Marks & Spencer fashion show, 1960s.

Michael News in 1955 was held at the Manchester Free Trade Hall and was attended by 2,000 people. The show resulted in a large number of enquiries about specific clothing merchandise which, in the majority of cases, resulted in a sale (*St Michael News*, 28 October 1955: 1). *The Northern Daily Telegraph* praised the show: 'Full marks for the simple but versatile styles … Full marks for jumpers with a zip at the back of the neck … Full marks for the suits in double jersey – certainly a very useful buy. These days winter woollies spell F-A-S-H-I-O-N' (quoted in ibid.).

By the end of the 1950s, Marks & Spencer had held more than thirty-five fashion shows to a total audience of 30,000. As well as creating publicity for the Marks & Spencer product, they were increasingly being used as money-raising events for charity (*St Michael News*, January 1959: 3).[7] By the 1970s, these shows had become highly organized, some touring the country for several months at a time (*St Michael News*, June 1976: 2). In 1995, a 'Marks & Spencer Live' roadshow toured for five weeks, performing at seventeen different venues to a total audience of 60,000 people, and was targeted primarily at existing charge card account holders.[8]

The first fashion show given by Marks & Spencer specifically for the press took place in 1965. Presented by Hans Schneider, head of the design department, this event, and the many others that took place subsequently, reveal the increasing importance to the high-street retailer of ensuring adequate and favourable press coverage in what was becoming an increasingly competitive high-street context. In 1985, Marks & Spencer held the first press show specifically for lingerie, reflecting the fashionable reputation earned by this huge department.

Rather more 'low key' were the exhibitions held in the 1950s, which performed primarily an educational role and their significance can be evaluated in the context of Marks & Spencer's post-war expansion of stores and against a background of rapid diversification of the clothing product. Two exhibitions organized by the company in 1956 illustrate this point admirably. The subject of the first exhibition was the modernization of Marks & Spencer stores after the Second World War, illustrating that between 1951 and 1955 over 17.7 km (11 miles) had been added to the company's counter-footage (*St Michael News*, 15 February 1956: 3). The aim of the second exhibition was to explain the different qualities of leather and plastic. Some visitors to the exhibition apparently confused leather handbags with plastic ones. The coverage devoted to this point by *St Michael News* was in itself a way of promoting plastic at a time when the company was beginning to use plastic as a replacement material for leather (*St Michael News*, 16 January 1956: 1). However, while these exhibitions performed an important function in the context of the 1950s, the most appropriate venues for 'educating the customer' (and which Marks & Spencer management believed provided the most diverse opportunities for selling the Marks & Spencer product) were the stores themselves.

THE MARKS & SPENCER STORE

The stores are the beginning and the end of our business. (I. Sieff)[9]

In the 1930s, Marks & Spencer had developed the policy of requiring all management recruits to head office (other than technologists) to spend two years in stores first. The store attachment was considered to be of paramount importance for the training of management recruits for head office in the areas of selection and merchandising, and continued with the advent of a graduate management-training scheme. This reflects the significance consigned by Marks & Spencer to the business of all the activities taking place in stores. Specifically, it revealed the belief that those undertaking the design – defined in the broadest sense – of the products to be sold in stores must have a detailed knowledge of the customer and the store environment. Even after the final selection and production of ranges, selectors and merchandisers were required to visit stores on a regular basis to talk to store managers and sales staff about the merchandise and to ascertain a qualitative appraisal of how ranges were selling (quantitative analyses were, of course, available via the checking lists and sales figures at head office).

As we have already seen, the company underwent a number of concentrated periods of expansion of its business, often accompanied by changes in strategy both in terms of the product itself and the manner in which the product was sold. For example, expansion of the Penny Bazaars before the First World War pivoted on the penny price point and the introduction and wide dissemination of the principle of self-selection, which, as Israel Sieff observed, would become one of the most important tenets of mid-twentieth-century retailing (I. Sieff 1970: 57). The company's expansion during the inter-war period went hand in hand with an emphasis on the 'new' Marks & Spencer product – clothing. Surviving photographs of intricate window displays in the 1930s (Fig. 27) reveal the importance at this time of attracting customers by ensuring that clothing had a strong visual impact.

The reconstruction of the business after the dislocation of the Second World War and the demise of the Utility clothing scheme afforded new opportunities for store expansion: in the decade after the war, total selling space was more than doubled and the marketing of new kinds of clothing, specifically those made from the new synthetic fabrics, was instrumental in the targeting of new kinds of customers. Specifically, the introduction of synthetic fabrics was integral to selling to a middle-

27: Window display, Blackpool store, 1938.

class customer as well as to the company's long-standing working-class customer. The need for the dissemination of information about new products made the adoption of media advertising more relevant than hitherto. The 1950s also saw the gradual removal of in-store cafeterias in order to make space for the display of clothing, with the aim of increasing the turnover of stock per square foot of selling space. Certainly this was achieved at the flagship Marble Arch store in London, which by 1974 (following the completion of a major extension in 1970 doubling its previous size) had entered the *Guinness Book of Records*, boasting the world's most profitable selling space. This was the store, *St Michael News* reported proudly, 'with the fastest-moving stock in the world' (*St Michael News*, July 1974: 6). Another extension was subsequently added in 1986, giving the store a total of four sales floors. Indeed, for the company as a whole, the most dynamic period of growth in the second half of the twentieth century – both in terms of the number of stores and changes in sales strategies – was, in many respects, the 1980s.

Of particular significance was the development, in the 1980s, of Marks & Spencer's first edge-of-town stores, the first opening in 1986 at the Metro Centre near Gateshead. By 1990, a fifth had been opened at Meadowhall near Sheffield. Accompanying these developments, the company announced in 1986 the 'biggest modernization programme since the 1960s': more than eighty stores were to be involved, a number of satellite stores were planned, and a total of thirty-two stores were to be given extended footage.[10]

What was happening at Marks & Spencer in the 1980s was in some respects a microcosm of retailing in general – there had been a shift away from an emphasis on the importance of manufacturing to, as Frank Mort observes, 'the sites of exchange':

> Sir Terence Conran [chairman of The Storehouse Group] argued that merchandising systems were now the most important component of any company. It was the point of sale, methods of stock control and delivery schedules, which mattered quite as much as the actual manufacture of commodities. (Mort 1996: 3–4)

The physical expansion of Marks & Spencer during the 1980s was accompanied by a rethinking of the image projected to the public through in-store design and layout, as well as a renewed emphasis on the importance of display. But just as Marks & Spencer had, since the days of the Penny Bazaars, invested the site of exchange of merchandise with the utmost importance, so does the attention given to display in this period need to be considered in a longer historical perspective.

DISPLAY

> Display is more forceful than newspaper advertising because the public see the actual article displayed. (Briggs 1984: 58)

Frank Mort has shown how, until the 1950s, the approach of the menswear retailer, Burton's, to commercial communications was conceived in local terms. Thus, window display, the role of the salesperson, and the location of the store on the high street, together with announcements in the regional press, were seen as the most effective forms of promotional culture (Mort 1997: 20). In the 1950s and 1960s, however, there was a dramatic reorganization of the retailer's advertising with a move away from local to national campaigns (Mort 1996: 140).[11] This pattern was broadly similar at Marks & Spencer.

The post-war period, as we have seen, ushered in a new phase in the way in which Marks & Spencer promoted its clothing. This was due largely to the need to spread the news about the qualities of the new synthetic fabrics, and to keep customers abreast of developments in terms of the reconstruction and expansion of the business following wartime dislocation and the demise of the Utility clothing scheme. Until this time, Marks & Spencer's approach to advertising (broadly defined) had been characterized by the belief that the product, if it was the right product, sold itself. This attitude helps to explain the emphasis placed by the company (prior to Marks & Spencer's employment of media advertising, from the 1950s) on the importance of window displays. The Marks & Spencer Archive holds a comprehensive collection of images of intricate window displays, spanning the 1930s to the 1960s (for example, Figs 1, 10, 11, 13, 19, 20 and 27). Companies such as Burton's also consigned great importance to the window display: it was the tangible reality of commodities on display that was the major selling asset. Even during the 1950s, 'traditional techniques of retailing', explains Mort, 'remained central for many firms during this period of consumer modernization' (ibid.).[12]

At Marks & Spencer, the role of in-store display had been nothing if not utilitarian until the 1970s and 1980s. In the 1980s, however, the company began to concentrate particularly on the way clothing was displayed and promoted in stores. To some extent, the developments described below can be regarded as a response by the company in order to keep abreast of the competition on the high street from clothing retailers such as Next (launched 1981) and Principles (launched 1984), combined with a rather disappointing performance in clothing in the mid-1980s relative to the other areas of the business such as homeware (introduced in 1986). In May 1985, although chairman Lord Rayner was able to announce record sales for the company as a whole, the sales of clothing had increased by only 7.4 per cent compared with an increase of 22.4 per cent for homeware and 14.6 per cent for foods (*St Michael News*, May 1985: 1). Nevertheless, of all the different product areas, clothing still accounted for the greatest volume of sales.

Such factors provided an incentive to instigate new ranges and new methods of display. The concept of the 'shop within a shop' was evolved: for example the lingerie 'shop', first trialled at the Hemel Hempstead store, sold the new lingerie collections (see Chapter 3). Stores were effectively redesigned in terms of creating 'walkways' and 'islands' on which coordinated merchandise could be displayed, along with more effective lighting and promotional photography. Walkways were designed to help steer the customer around the store so that particular displays of merchandise would have maximum impact, at the same time guiding the customer towards increasingly coordinated ranges of clothing (Fig. 28).

The idea of displaying coordinating garments was by no means new in the 1980s, but there was a refinement of the concept through more formalized display techniques. A trial display of men's casual wear (in which coordinating shorts and jogging outfits were displayed together to enable customers to assemble outfits with ease and to encourage multiple sales) proved to be particularly successful (*St Michael News*, May 1984: 7). Menswear also followed the example of a successful display technique in womenswear with the introduction of a 'beach bar' in which men's shorts and swimming trunks were displayed alongside sunglasses, towels and sun lotions (*St Michael News*, April 1986: 1). In addition, new kinds of lighting techniques and mannequins were introduced into stores, as well as specially designed racks on which the merchandise could be displayed for maximum impact.

In the 1980s, the sales promotion department devised, for the first time, coordinated themes in which selected merchandise was to be promoted at a specific time by all stores. In 1987, the concept of the 'colour theme' was introduced into

28: Bromley store, *St Michael News*, January 1986.

womenswear. Working in tandem, the buying and design departments put together a number of successive colour promotions to be introduced into stores in order to stimulate customers' interest throughout the season. This became more sophisticated during the 1990s as not only additional colours, but also different ranges of merchandise, were introduced in phases throughout the selling season in order to encourage customers to keep returning to see the latest clothing (Fig. 29).

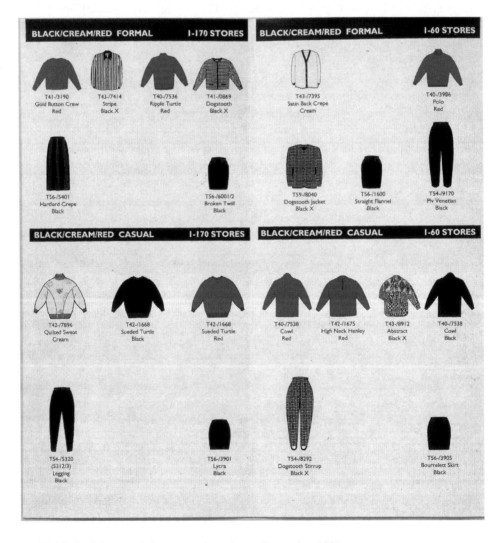

29: Marks & Spencer ladieswear colour theme, September 1991.

These developments may be seen as the forerunners of more far-reaching changes in merchandising in the 1990s. Following initiatives in menswear, in 1996 the whole of womenswear was divided into 'casual' and 'formal' 'packages' (rather than by individual product) for the purposes of coordination and display.

QUALITY SERVICE

In 1981 Marks & Spencer embarked upon a 'good service' or 'Welcome to Marks & Spencer' campaign, designed to offer the customer a better in-store service. This was followed by the introduction of a 'Quality Service' campaign in 1988. As part of the latter, a bra-measuring service (advertised on the *Clothes Show*) and a suit-ordering service were launched (*St Michael News*, May 1988: 7). On one level, this initiative can be seen in the context of the appearance of stores such as Next and Gap on the high street, both of which made good customer service a priority. On another level, it can be seen in a longer historical perspective, and as a more formalized expression of a long-established policy. For example, in 1972 an eight-page colour supplement appeared in *Woman's Own*, recommending St Michael bras and girdles. In a question and answer format, advice was given illustrating the right foundation garment for individual figure 'problems'. This coincided with coordinated events taking place in stores. At Wood Green (north London), for example, there were special training sessions for staff so that they could help customers to choose the correct garments more effectively. In addition, special window displays, ticketing and wall banners were introduced (*St Michael News*, April 1972: 5). Other innovations were also designed to improve the service given to the customer. In the early 1970s, for example, the concept of self-selection was partly replaced by that of 'assisted self-selection': sales assistants were not only expected to operate the till but to maintain displays and, most importantly of all, to assist customers in their purchases of clothing by helping to find the required size or colour (*St Michael News*, August 1971: 2).

Significantly, Marks & Spencer's concept of quality service was not only about providing a service, but a way of 'educating the customer'. Swing tickets began to be used at Marks & Spencer from at least the mid-1950s. Sold along with the garment to which they were attached, these conveyed important information about, for example, the nature of the fabric (this also provided a useful means of promotion for the fabric producer), and the method of application of decoration if appropriate (for example a 'hand-embroidered' or 'hand-smocked' garment). They might also give particular washing instructions. For example, in 1955, swing tickets, along with special store showcards, were being used to promote wool in the form of a baby lamb motif (*St Michael News*, 10 June 1955: 1). Swing tickets appeared on Bri-Nylon knitwear in the early 1960s, with information regarding 'tried and tested washing instructions' (*St Michael News*, January 1961: 2). As Marks & Spencer developed into an international business, these swing tickets began to include information translated into different languages. Besides swing tickets, special free leaflets were made available to customers on subjects such as 'Taking Care of Knitwear' (1997).

As this chapter has illustrated, by 'quality service' Marks & Spencer meant not only the intrinsic quality of the goods, but also the service provided both before, during and after a sale had been made. This included the information given about the product in order to inform the purchase of clothing (through advertising and swing tickets), advice given about caring for garments, and the provision of a favourable exchange and refund policy. Quality service would also be affected by the shopping 'environment' – be it a store or, from 1998, mail-order catalogue ('Marks & Spencer Direct') or, from 1999, online shopping.[13] As Marks & Spencer evolved into an international business during the 1980s and 1990s, the company had to reassess some of its sales strategies in the light of diverse cultural and shopping practices. Some of the most significant of these will be considered in Chapter 5 in so far as they impacted upon the clothing sold by Marks & Spencer and helped to redefine the nature of fashion in an increasingly international context in the late twentieth century. Furthermore, the diverse ways in which Marks & Spencer sold clothing helped to enhance the perceived quality of its merchandise and make the customer more knowledgeable in terms of, for example, caring for a product and therefore ensuring its longevity. Arguably, while quality clothing that was 'made to last' was traditionally sought by the 'discerning' customer, the advent of a more rapid turn-around in fashion (both in terms of the apparently insatiable desire for something new on the part of the customer, and the advancement of technological capabilities to produce new styles and colours in order to continually inject novelty on the high street) made the Marks & Spencer philosophy anachronistic to some extent. The way Marks & Spencer responded to the changing retailing environment in the 1990s reflects in some measure changing definitions of fashion and gives an interesting perspective on what constitutes democratization in the context of fashion spanning international boundaries.

We have established M&S as a truly international retailer.
Lord Rayner, *St Michael News*, Christmas Issue 1989

From the 1970s, Marks & Spencer extended its influence in an international direction, boasting a retail presence in 683 locations worldwide by 1998 (*Company Facts* 1998), thus giving the concept of the democratization of fashion a new, 'global' perspective. It was Marks & Spencer's growing international presence that had prompted Whitebloom to proclaim in *The Guardian* in 1996 that: 'The way Marks is going, it will literally soon be possible to encircle the world in green plastic carrier bags (18 October 1996: 22). In spite of the fact that by the start of the twenty-first century, the company was declaring not only a halt to its international expansion but also the closure of what had been key stores abroad, such as the one on Boulevard Haussmann, Paris, the long-term impact of expansion by clothing retailers outside their country of origin was to stimulate the fashion industry (like many others in the last decades of the twentieth century) to undergo a complex process of globalization, both in the production and consumption of clothing. Marks & Spencer's international expansion needs of course to be seen in the context of a more pervasive globalization of the fashion market at all levels, from haute couture to high-street chains, with US clothing companies such as Gap pioneering this trend.

This chapter discusses Marks & Spencer's international expansion in terms of the company's sourcing policies, export business, and franchises and stores established abroad. Finally, it will discuss the impact of increasing internationalization on the clothing product itself. In general terms, the company's international expansion caused the company to review a number of its UK sales strategies, as well as its clothing ranges, thereby influencing the way the British public shopped and the clothing they bought. It also affected concepts of shopping and fashion in the 'host' countries. The company's assessment of consumers' needs and behaviour in the countries where it had ambitions for expansion led in some cases to a revision of its policies for its UK stores too, for example concerning the provision of fitting rooms. In 1978, Marks & Spencer explained why it was necessary for the then three-year-old Boulevard Haussmann store in Paris to have twenty-four fitting rooms: 'This is because we have so few stores [in France] at the moment and a customer might have to travel some distance in order to change a garment' (*St Michael News*, December 1978: 1). It was also a case of acknowledging different shopping practices: the

French shopper would be unlikely to buy an item of clothing without first trying it on. Significantly, the introduction of fitting rooms in Marks & Spencer's Continental stores prompted the company to introduce them in the UK (see Chapter 4).

While Marks & Spencer 'imported' into its UK stores policies it had introduced initially only in its stores abroad, it also 'exported' established UK Marks & Spencer retail practices (exchange and refund policies, for example, discussed in Chapter 4). This 'cross-fertilization' also impacted on the actual product sold: as Marks & Spencer pointed out in 1978, 'Stores in the UK are already selling French-made rain-coats, ladies' suits and skirts, as well as food' (ibid.). Meanwhile, in France, a fashion column in *Le Figaro* eulogized about a chenille cardigan *à la Chanel* on sale in Marks & Spencer's Boulevard Haussmann store for a fraction of the price of the designer version (*St Michael News*, October 1981: 3). This mostly positive, reciprocal relationship between the Marks & Spencer UK and worldwide businesses made a significant contribution to the internationalization of fashion by the late twentieth century.

Combined with the ongoing communications revolution via the media and the Internet, the upshot of the expansion abroad of retail chains such as Marks & Spencer was that fashion and the way clothing was manufactured and acquired became an increasingly international business. While there were still, of course, considerable acknowledged differences within the global clothing market, by the 1990s, the similarities appeared to many to be even more striking. Indeed, if this was not the case, it would have been extremely difficult for Marks & Spencer to have achieved the level of expansion abroad as things stood in the mid-1990s.[1] However, the subsequent closure of stores abroad is a reminder that simplistic models of a completely international consumer market are inadequate.

SOURCING

The concept of an international market may be described both in terms of where goods are produced (sourced) and where they are retailed. In the case of Marks & Spencer's sourcing policies, these changed markedly over the period identified in this study, broadly reflecting the transition the company made from being primarily a British concern to one which by the 1990s could more accurately (at least superficially) be described in global terms. In 1996, Derek Hayes, director for European retail operations at Marks & Spencer, stressed the importance of trying to manufacture close to the markets in which the company was operating, not simply to make distribution easier, but also because of the imperative of employing local people (*Drapers Record*, 23 March 1996: 12).

The seeds of Marks and Spencer's sourcing policy were sown in the 1930s. For example, before Hitler's rise to power, Germany had been Marks & Spencer's largest supplier of artificial silk fully fashioned hosiery. After 1933, however, Marks &

Spencer found an alternative supplier in Czechoslovakia and later France. Nevertheless, in 1939, 94 per cent of Marks & Spencer merchandise sold in stores was still of British manufacture (I. Sieff, 1970: 156). Furthermore, wartime dislocation meant that Britain could not rely on imports from abroad and by the late 1950s, this figure had risen to 99 per cent.[2] On the whole, until the mid-1980s it was Marks & Spencer's policy to buy British whenever possible.

Supporting the British textile and clothing industries, at an extremely difficult time for both, was very much a part of the philosophy of Lord (Marcus) Sieff, chairman from 1972 until 1984. In the early 1980s, Marks & Spencer's policy as stated by Lord Sieff was as follows: 'We only buy from abroad when we cannot find good quality and value at home. We have encouraged our foreign suppliers, particularly food suppliers, not to process their high-quality raw materials in their home country, but to set up new plants in Britain' (St Michael News, November 1982: 1). The company considered this policy to be part and parcel of a social responsibility it owed to its suppliers, staff and customers if it was to maintain its market edge, not to mention jobs.[3]

From the 1970s, the opening of Marks & Spencer stores abroad highlighted the potential benefits of sourcing clothing from abroad and would eventually mark a shift in the company's sourcing policies. Marks & Spencer not only encouraged UK-based suppliers to venture abroad, but also utilized suppliers already located overseas to supply its foreign retail outlets. Thus although Marks & Spencer's Canadian stores obtained merchandise such as knitwear and lingerie from British suppliers, over 70 per cent of goods were sourced locally by 1977 (St Michael News, July 1976: 7 and February 1977: 7).[4] In the case of the company's expansion in the Far East, from the late 1980s – the first Marks & Spencer stores in the Far East were opened in Hong Kong's Kowloon in 1988 – the growth of retail operations went hand in hand with the development of Asia as a sourcing centre (M&S World, Winter 1990–91: 25). At about the same time, a buying office was established in Hong Kong to find new sources of merchandise to serve Marks & Spencer customers' needs both in the Far East and worldwide (St Michael News, November 1987: 8).

Thus, in spite of the stated policy of selling British-made goods, it was becoming increasingly obvious to some Marks & Spencer personnel, even as early as the start of the 1980s, that the textile industry 'had to become more international in concept' and that in certain cases, Marks & Spencer would have to go abroad to ensure 'we get the best quality and value or because the product or technology is not available to us in this country' (Underwood, 1981, Marks & Spencer Archive). By the late 1980s, the advantages of sourcing from abroad were becoming clear. In 1989, some 87 per cent of all clothing sold by Marks & Spencer was made in Britain, not perhaps a noticeable decrease by comparison with the figure of a decade before, but very much the start of a new trend (St Michael News, July 1989: 1). This change in policy coincided with the beginning of a major period of retail expansion abroad for Marks

& Spencer. Both developments necessitated a reassessment and diversification of the Marks & Spencer clothing product.

MARKS & SPENCER'S EXPORT BUSINESS

In 1977, Marks & Spencer was awarded the Queen's Award for Export following a two-year period (1975–77) during which the company's exports trebled, rising from a total value of £13.5 million to £40 million (Briggs 1984:14). This figure had risen substantially since the mid-1950s, when Marks & Spencer was exporting goods to the value of £703,000 (ibid.: 117). Although the 1970s figures represent a marked increase over a short period of time, the growth of the company's export business nevertheless needs to be seen in evolutionary and organic terms. The origins of Marks & Spencer's export trade go back to the Second World War, when Israel Sieff was invited by the Board of Trade to go to the USA with the aim, observes Rees, of promoting and expanding British exports in order to generate American dollars and thus help finance the war effort. As a result of Sieff's negotiations, the Marks & Spencer Export Corporation was set up in 1940 and provided the Treasury with $10 million from the sale of British textiles and clothing (Rees 1973: 169). As Paul Bookbinder notes, this was the company's first exercise in bulk exporting (Bookbinder 1993: 125).

However, substantial development of Marks & Spencer's export trade really dates from the period of reconstruction after the Second World War. In 1955, an article in *St Michael News*, unambiguously entitled 'The World Shops at M&S' drew attention to the large number of requests for Marks & Spencer merchandise from abroad, underlining the company's future potential in this area (*St Michael News*, 7 October 1955: 2). By the late 1950s, Marks & Spencer was exporting clothing to countries such as Ghana and Nigeria (*St Michael News*, June 1958: 1). An exhibition at head office – 'Export 1964–65' – illustrated that Marks & Spencer had 'established the St Michael brand in over sixty countries throughout the world' (*St Michael News*, January/February 1965: 1). Furthermore, Marks & Spencer estimated that, by the mid-1960s, 'the extent of foreign custom at the Marble Arch store is 50 per cent of total sales' (*St Michael News*, October 1966: 8). Fashion shows were held for direc-tors and buying executives from leading stores in thirty countries, as part of what may be described as a concerted export drive (*St Michael News*, June 1965: 1). The popu-larity of Marks & Spencer lingerie abroad was reflected in special lingerie fashion shows for export customers, the first of which was held in 1979 (*St Michael News*, November 1979: 1). The success of Marks & Spencer's export trade established that there was an untapped market (beyond the company's familiar territory) for Marks & Spencer goods. In many respects, this was the forerunner of further expansion – the establishment of franchises and the opening of stores abroad.

One of the ways in which Marks & Spencer developed its business abroad was through building up franchises. In 1997, Marks & Spencer had a total of eighty-five (franchise) shops in twenty countries worldwide. In the late 1970s, *St Michael* merchandise was sold by the Japanese retailer Daiei Inc., for example (*St Michael News*, October 1978: 3), and was orchestrated by the export group at head office. By the late 1980s, this had been replaced by the international franchise group, with the first of a 'new generation' of franchise operations opening in Lisbon in 1988. In this and in other Marks & Spencer franchises opened subsequently, the Marks & Spencer image was reproduced using the same pattern of walkways, lighting and displays as those found in UK stores (*M&S World*, Autumn 1989: 20).

As an article in *M&S World* explained, the aim of the franchise was to establish important new markets without any capital investment and to work more closely with existing customers to maintain the company's standards. According to Marks & Spencer export manager Roy Bannister, 'Franchising [is] a formalization of what our [export] customers [are] doing, creating an internationally acceptable look and a management structure and style of operation reflecting the best in the UK' (ibid.). Thus, franchise agreements often grew out of relationships already established between Marks & Spencer and export customers. In Hong Kong, for example, the establishment of a franchise was the first step towards the company opening its own stores there: Marks & Spencer merchandise was sold via a franchise agreement with the Dodwell store chain well before the first stores opened in Kowloon. Similarly, in Spain, St Michael clothing could be bought in the department stores Galerias Preciados prior to the opening of the first store in Madrid in 1990.

In 1998, Marks & Spencer had eighty-seven stores outside the UK: Belgium (4), France (20), the Netherlands (2), Republic of Ireland (3), Spain (7), Hong Kong (10), Canada (43), and Germany (1).[5] The opening of the first Marks & Spencer stores abroad in the 1970s can be seen as a direct development from the already well-established export trade, considered above. For example, when in 1972 the first store in Canada was opened in Brampton near Toronto, the company had already been involved in the export of goods to Canada for approximately thirty years. Marks & Spencer's original decision to move into Europe with a chain of wholly owned stores was taken after Britain joined the EEC in 1973. In 1975, the first store opened in France in the prestigious Parisian shopping street, Boulevard Haussmann, and was situated opposite the well-known French department stores of Printemps and Galeries Lafayette – 'perhaps', Lord (Marcus) Sieff noted with understandable caution, 'the Paris equivalents of Harrods and Selfridges' (M. Sieff 1988: 298). These initiatives were not immediate or unmitigated successes, however. According to Sieff, the most serious mistake made by Marks & Spencer in the initial opening of stores abroad in the 1970s was that the company 'exported' its UK policies without taking into account local conditions:

> In general our mistake overseas has been our failure to modify policy to suit local conditions. We believed that our British policies and practices would work just as well abroad as at home; we were wrong, and we have learned from our mistakes. In fact, the lessons we have learned in Canada and France have relevance to our developments in the United Kingdom, and are being applied successfully here. (M. Sieff 1988: 300)

Initial experiences in France, recalls Sieff, were not dissimilar to those in Canada and one of the specific 'lessons' learned was the importance of fitting rooms (discussed above) for customers who might have travelled some distance to visit the store (M. Sieff: 1988: 298–9). More generally, Marks & Spencer soon recognized the necessity of in-depth, painstaking market research of local trading conditions (including obtaining a database of information on customers, retailers and products) before an attempt was made to open a store in a new country. The benefit of such research was illustrated by the success of the first store openings in Spain (1990) and in Germany (1996).

When interviewed in the mid-1990s, Alan Lambert, divisional director for European merchandise perceived it thus: that the major difference between Marks & Spencer's operations in the UK and those in France was the length of time the company had been established in the respective countries, and all that this implied (Interview with Alan Lambert, 18 December 1995). Abroad, Marks & Spencer could not rely on the long-established reputation for good quality and value enjoyed in the UK, and herein lay the challenge when expanding outside the UK. In Germany, for example, Clive Nickolds, divisional director for European operations, was reported to have observed, 'The St Michael name is unknown', adding, somewhat patronizingly, 'We will have to educate the Germans about it' (*Draper's Record, DR Focus*, 7 September 1996: viii). In 1995, the then deputy chairman Keith Oates highlighted the need for Marks & Spencer to have a similar image – in terms of the value of its merchandise – both abroad and in the UK. Indeed, Marks & Spencer was said to have taken a cut in the level of their profit margins in order to achieve this (Cowe, *The Guardian*, 28 March 1995: 15).

Thus, changes in the company's advertising policies from the mid-1970s (see Chapter 4) can be seen to some extent in the context of Marks & Spencer's desire to shape its foreign customers' perceptions both of the company and of the products it sold, and indeed advertising became crucially important in order to promote the Marks & Spencer 'message'. According to an article in *St Michael News*, only 3 per cent of the population had heard of Marks & Spencer in Paris and Brussels prior to the opening of the first stores there (*St Michael News*, February 1975: 8). Advertisements such as one whose slogan read, '"Le Shopping" c'est Marks & Spencer' appeared in French and Belgian newspapers and magazines. In Paris, as well as advertisements published in *Le Monde, Le Figaro, Elle* and *Paris Match*, some 4,500 posters made their way on to Parisian buses and 450 on to the Metro (ibid.). The company's expansion abroad thus affected strategies for selling fashion, but equally significant was the impact on the clothing itself.

THE IMPACT OF INTERNATIONAL EXPANSION ON THE MARKS & SPENCER CLOTHING PRODUCT

> Tastes in fashion and food are becoming more alike and best-sellers in the UK are equally popular in the rest of Europe, in the Far East and in North America.
> (Keith Oates, deputy chairman, *M&S World*, Winter 1995: 2)

In 1989, an international office was established at Marks & Spencer's head office in Baker Street to coordinate the company's huge expansion overseas (*St Michael News*, Summer 1990: 3). The objective was to work with the company's offices abroad, such as the one in Hong Kong set up to coordinate Marks & Spencer's retail links not only with Hong Kong but with Asia generally, including operations in Singapore and the Philippines. Liaison between offices, it was hoped, would ensure that effective cataloguing, distribution, pricing and sourcing of goods for local markets could be achieved and that sales information fed back to UK departments, thereby developing a more rapid and accurate response to international fashion trends.

When Marks & Spencer opened the first stores in Canada in the early 1970s, the clothing sold was a specially selected range of merchandise chosen from the UK ranges, although this policy would change by the end of the decade (but see also Note 4). Similarly, in the late 1980s, 90 per cent of the clothing merchandise sold in European stores was selected from the ranges already developed for the UK business. Notwithstanding the fact that garments and ranges purchased directly for Marks & Spencer's Continental stores – 'European specials' – were starting to account for a growing percentage of the merchandise sold,[6] the company continued to sell broadly the same offer worldwide, albeit taking into account regional cultural and climatic differences when constructing the catalogue for a particular city or country. Moreover, perceived cultural dissimilarities were sometimes used to Marks & Spencer's advantage. For example, in the mid-1970s, particular French favourites were often those garments associated with 'Britishness': traditional cashmere pullovers, Shetland sweaters and pure wool skirts, for example (*St Michael News*, December 1977: 1).[7]

Significantly, in 1994, the best-selling item in Marks & Spencer's Hong Kong stores was a women's blazer inspired by a Brooks Brothers version (*St Michael News*, March 1990: 2) which, according to an article in *The M&S Magazine*, 'must be the fastest-selling ladies' item of clothing in the world' (*The M&S Magazine*, Spring 1994: 83) (Fig. 23). Styles such as these, which seemed to sell well wherever in the world they were retailed, led to the assumption that if a particular garment or range of garments sold well in Manchester, it was likely also to be a best-seller in Madrid. Indeed, the sales figures seemed to support such a conclusion.

Therefore, in the 1990s, the main differences in consumer demand seemed to be those of sizing, fabric (affected by climate) and colour. Just as certain areas of the UK always had different requirements from other areas, many of these differences revolved around merchandising issues rather than hinging on the nature of the intrinsic product. The crucial importance of getting the right size ratios is a good example of this: in 1996, *Draper's Record* reported that Germany required a size ratio in which larger sizes predominated and Marks & Spencer increased the size range in key lines to accommodate the larger German frame (*Drapers Record, DR Focus*, 7 September 1996: viii). Marks & Spencer's Hong Kong stores, on the other hand, would require special (smaller) size blocks (Anon., 9 November 1983, Marks & Spencer Archive). In Spain in the mid-1990s, shorter skirt lengths were sold, not only because the average Spaniard is shorter than the average Briton, but also because Spanish fashion demanded that skirts were worn shorter.

Colour, on the other hand, Marks & Spencer personnel believed, was becoming increasingly 'internationalized' – notwithstanding the fact that the company acknowledged that Spain would typically sell more greens, olives and browns than the UK whereas France would sell more navy blue. In Hong Kong, red sold particularly well. However, the 'top six' best-selling colours across the Marks & Spencer business worldwide were the same, albeit in a different order (*M&S World*, Winter 1990–91: 8). Perhaps this is not surprising considering the international influence of the fashion prediction business and the significance for fashion buyers and retailers of the colour palette exhibited at trade and fabric fairs such as Première Vision.

Just as Marcus Sieff commented retrospectively on the company's international expansion of the 1970s and acknowledged that to assume that Marks & Spencer's policies could be 'exported' wholesale was misguided (see above), Hans Schneider, head of the design department (see Chapter 3) wrote to the chairman about the importance of Marks & Spencer making an 'up-to-date impression … by Continental standards' when choosing appropriate merchandise for the company's planned French and Belgian stores. He made the following observation in a memo to the chairman, Marcus Sieff:

> Although I accept that the merchandise in our UK stores must form the back-bone of the Continental catalogue, it must be realized that the penetration of fashion throughout the Continental retail trade, from the most expensive shops to the small boutiques and the chain and multiple stores, is much more thorough than in England. Continental customers, especially the French, accept new trends immediately. (Hans Schneider to Marcus Sieff, 5 November 1973, Marks & Spencer Archive)

Schneider went on to recommend the following: 'We should consider very seriously the possibility of filling a part of our Continental catalogue by purchases from Continental manufacturers, who are more aware of trends and have quicker access to new fabrics and up-to-date colourings. I hope and expect that such an effort would also be beneficial to our fashion ranges in the UK' (ibid.).

Judging from the influence that Schneider had at Marks & Spencer, it seems reasonable to assume that his advice was heeded and that expansion abroad subsequently contributed both to the reassessment of the design element of the ranges of clothing sold, as well as to the company's corporate image and identity already discussed in Chapters 3 and 4 respectively. Such discussions within Marks & Spencer reflect the company's quest for a more 'internationally appealing' fashionable image. Thus, Marks & Spencer's successful expansion abroad can be seen as both cause and effect of the steadily increasing internationalization of the fashion business in the last quarter of the twentieth century.

Marks & Spencer's international expansion resulted in the diversification of the clothing ranges sold in the UK and abroad, while at the same time contributing to a reassessment of the Marks & Spencer image, projected at least partly by particular sales strategies. In Hong Kong, for example, carrier bags with cord handles were introduced to give the Marks & Spencer product a more 'upmarket' image than the one conferred by the green plastic bags utilized in the UK. Marks & Spencer's acquisition of the Brooks Brothers chain in the USA in 1988 (along with the store's classic image) resulted in significant additions to the UK clothing ranges. The men's button-down shirt is a case in point. In 1989, *GQ* announced the arrival of the original Brooks Brothers button-down shirt in London's Marks & Spencer stores (*GQ*, October/November 1989). In addition, Brooks's practice of selling men's suits with wider seams and hems that were left unfinished (should customers need some alteration) was partly 'transferred' to the UK business with the introduction of an alteration service – albeit on a smaller scale – into eighty stores in the early 1990s (*M&S World*, Autumn/Winter 1993–94: 4). Conversely, and at the same time, Brooks Brothers began to include merchandise from the Marks & Spencer ranges, for example women's cotton crew-neck sweaters, which were popular in the UK, were sold on a trial basis under the Brooks Brothers label in the USA (ibid.).

The significance of Marks & Spencer's contribution to the global clothing market is well illustrated by the international success of the company's lingerie ranges, which achieved 30 per cent of clothing sales in Marks & Spencer's overseas business in 1990–91 (*M&S World*, Winter 1990–91: 9). The Boulevard Haussmann store in Paris proved to be the company's second most successful outlet for lingerie in 1992 (Glaister, *The Guardian*, 15 December 1992: 12–13), while in Spain, according to an article in *Draper's Record*, Marks & Spencer helped to shape local requirements by 'almost single-handedly chang[ing] women's lingerie-buying habits away from branded bras to own label (*Draper's Record*, 23 March 1996: 12).

To summarize, it may be argued that the degree to which fashion and the fashion business became internationalized by the end of the twentieth century – a process in which patterns of clothing consumption hitherto dictated primarily by tradition and cultural differences seemed to have become blurred and indistinct – appeared to be self-perpetuating. In 1993, it was reported that Marks & Spencer was accelerating its worldwide store development programme, with the objective of adding about 46,451 sq. metres (500,000 sq. ft), the equivalent of more than ten new stores in each of the subsequent three years (Wilkinson, *The Independent*, 4 November 1993: 37). Shortly afterwards, the company announced the opening of an office in Shanghai, with the aim of building links with government and local businesses for possible expansion into China. New franchise agreements were forged in Turkey and Hungary and, in 1996, Marks & Spencer announced the opening of a (franchise) store in Prague, while the first store in Germany opened in the autumn of the same year.[8]

It is perhaps ironic that shortly before the downturn in Marks & Spencer's profits, Roger Cowe observed in *The Guardian* in 1997: 'Stay at home or travel, there is no escape' from the Marks & Spencer success story (Cowe, *The Guardian*, 21 May 1997: 19). Significantly, however, Cowe also observed that a year previously, as much new space had been added in the UK as was opened elsewhere in the world. Although profits earned from Marks & Spencer's overseas business had seen an upturn – with the Far East being especially profitable, so far as 'contributions to record returns' were concerned – 'home is still best' with the UK the nerve centre of the entire Marks & Spencer business (ibid.). Thus, Marks & Spencer's halt to international expansion at the start of the twenty-first century and the closure of stores abroad begs the question of whether there can ever be a completely global market. But while it may have slowed down a process set in motion over thirty years previously, it did not necessarily reverse it.

> He [Simon Marks], more than any other man, was responsible for a democratic revolution in dress for the British woman. He made imaginative styles and good quality available to everyone instead of the few.
>
> Obituary for Lord Marks, *The Guardian*, 9 December 1964

> There was once a slogan printed on a well-known box of matches: 'It is better for the goods to bring back the customer than for the customer to bring back the goods'. That sums up the Marks & Spencer philosophy on quality and value.
>
> *St Michael News*, October 1976

Contrary to what the bias in fashion history literature would have us believe, fashion is not the exclusive preserve of the rich, but is of relevance and importance to the majority of people. Over the course of the twentieth century, increasing accessibility to well-designed and good-quality clothing for all social classes has widened the parameters and definition of what is generally understood by the term 'fashion'. Since the mid-1920s and 1930s, the multiple chain stores have played a key role in the democratization of fashion. This study has argued that Marks & Spencer has made a unique contribution.

After the Second World War, contemporaries commented on the way in which the actual manifestations of class differences, in terms of the way people dressed, were becoming less obvious:

> Before the Welfare State there were broadly two classes of consumers, the middle class, who had the money, and the working class, who hadn't. Now there is only one class; and I am told ... that many a debutante wears an M&S nylon slip beneath her Dior dress as if she were just a Gateshead factory girl. (Thompson, *News Chronicle*, 1955, quoted in Briggs 1984: 78)

While the language of Lawrence Thompson's observation betrays a post-war society which was still, in fact, overtly class-conscious, significantly it also acknowledges the way in which the manifestation of these social divisions could be eroded, at least in part, through the consumer's choice of dress, specifically the mixing of Marks & Spencer lingerie with a designer dress, even if the former was hidden by the latter. Furthermore, the association between the 'Gateshead factory girl' and Marks

& Spencer underwear is telling, of course, pointing to the working-class consumer originally targeted by Marks & Spencer (discussed in Chapter 1).

However, by the 1950s (some would argue as early as the late 1930s[1]), Marks & Spencer clothing appealed to the working classes as well as to those in a higher income bracket. Furthermore, Roberts observes that fashion itself was undermining class differences and creating a more homogeneous society, in which it was more difficult to assess people's status and occupation by the way they dressed (Roberts 1995: 14). Indeed, in the period after the Second World War, it was becoming increasingly difficult to define 'the working class' (ibid.: 237). Marks & Spencer's role, from the 1950s, in introducing the new synthetic fabrics – along with their classless appeal – certainly contributed to this process. Interestingly, by the 1960s, the term 'classless' was being associated with the Marks & Spencer retailing philosophy. Thus *The Guardian* claimed in 1965, 'Classless is a fair description of the giant organization which retails under the name of *St Michael*.[2] Israel Sieff observed that the company was both 'reflecting and, at the same time, helping to bring about, that *democratization* [my italics] of demand which was a feature of post-war Britain, and which invariably goes with, and again, helps bring about, a more egalitarian society' (I. Sieff 1970: 181). Acknowledging the way in which the retailer/producer and the customer/demand operated not in isolation but in tandem, it is significant that Sieff saw the impact of Marks & Spencer as both cause and effect of these changes.

Kawamura observes that in the twentieth century, fashion became increasingly democratic, and everyone, regardless of rank or status, had the right to look fashionable (Kawamura 2005: 5). While the term 'democratization' has thus been used to chart changes in fashion in the twentieth century, the process by which this has taken place has not been described in detail. However, in the context of this study it has been defined as the ability of an increasing number of people to have access to good-quality, well-designed and affordable clothing. Marks & Spencer enabled their customers to exert a larger measure of choice in this respect. Specifically, from the 1920s and 1930s onwards, there were two different, but related, processes at work. Firstly, Marks & Spencer made high-quality clothing at reasonable prices, which was available to those on low incomes and secondly, the company 'upgraded' the product (in terms of both quality and design) but still sold it at a fraction of the price of the clothing sold at the designer end of the market and, as we have seen, cheaper than that sold by Marks & Spencer's competitors such as C&A (see Chapter 1). This process began in the 1930s with the establishment of a textile laboratory (Chapter 2) and a design department (Chapter 3) but became more 'visible' in the 1980s and 1990s as Marks & Spencer reviewed its sales and advertising strategies in a highly competitive high-street context (Chapter 4). These factors resulted in an expansion of Marks & Spencer's share of the market, which in turn brought about a further levelling of the market in both social and economic terms.

Developments in the factory system producing ready-made clothing, particularly women's clothing, were relatively slow to make an impact on patterns of clothing consumption (Chapter 2). In fact, up until the outbreak of the First World War, only a very small proportion of the supply of women's clothes was ready-made (Fraser 1981: 179). The advent of the sewing machine in the mid-nineteenth century and the availability of paper patterns initially encouraged the home dressmaking trade. Furthermore, the 'shoddy trade' had tended to give ready-made clothing in general a reputation for poor quality, sometimes with justification. Consequently, when Marks & Spencer turned to the production of clothing on a large scale in the late 1920s and 1930s, it is easy to see why the emphasis on *quality* clothing constituted both a marketing coup as well as an expression of what became company 'philosophy', imbibed in the St Michael trademark (Chapter 4). The company was clearly responding to changes in market demand. Jeffreys, for example, has shown that in the first half of the twentieth century, although the proportion of total retail expenditure by consumers on clothing did not change greatly, the changes in the type of goods purchased were very marked, such that 'in the case of both the men's and the women's trade there was a shift from the purchase of piece goods for making up at home to the purchase of ready-made articles' (Jeffreys 1954: 294–5). Significantly, from the mid-1920s, Marks & Spencer's development as a business went hand in hand with the retailing of clothing.

From the late 1920s, the direct relationships the company had forged with its suppliers – encouraging long production runs and the avoidance of on-costs (costs added on to the garments) imposed by wholesalers (Chapter 2) – meant that Marks & Spencer could reduce the prices at which goods were retailed. One response to developments in the retailing of clothing can be seen in a report published by the Board of Trade in 1932 – an 'Industrial Survey of the Lancashire Area' – which stated that: 'Factory-made dresses can often be sold in the shops for less than the cost of the cloth bought in retail stores ... This has brought ready-made frocks within the reach of the majority of women and has compelled numbers of local dressmakers to go out of business.'[3] Although the dressmaker continued to play an important role into the 1950s, a feature in *The Housewife* in 1955 asking, 'Is there a future for the private dressmaker?' confirmed that the latter's role was clearly under threat. The article added that the high quality once only available from the private dressmaker was now to be had from chain stores such as Marks & Spencer (quoted in *St Michael News*, 1 July 1955: 4). Thus, by the 1950s, ready-made clothes were no longer necessarily associated with poor quality.

In summary, from the 1920s and 1930s, fashion was no longer the exclusive preserve of a wealthy minority. The clothing sold by Marks & Spencer not only appealed to a rapidly growing sector of the market but also helped to create that market. Furthermore, changing social roles for women in the period after the Second World War – for example, the gradual acceptance that women would go out to work and the introduction of labour-saving devices in the home – along with specific government-led initiatives such as the Utility clothing scheme (Chapter 2), gradually changed previous patterns of clothing demand and consumption. It was the explicit policy of Marks & Spencer to enable those families and individuals with less disposable income to 'spend on clothing to have access to good-quality, well-designed clothes. Although prices during the Second World War had been 'artificially' inflated, by the 1950s retailers were able to cater for a mass market by offering the customer cheaper staple goods, which in the case of Marks & Spencer were sold via a succession of lower-price 'campaigns' (discussed below). As Simon Marks observed in 1954:

> When some thirty years ago we entered the field of textiles, quality and beauty of garments were reserved for those of ample means. For the mass of the people, the clothing available was drab and of poor quality. The rise of the multiple shops displaying boots and shoes and all kinds of clothing produced by mass-production methods brought about great social changes. Men, women and children changed over to more practical and attractive garments, cheaper in price and better in quality. It is not without satisfaction that it can be said that Marks & Spencer had a prominent part in those social changes. (quoted in Bookbinder 1993: 138)

THE 1950S AND 1960S: 'NEW LOWER PRICES, QUALITY MAINTAINED'

During the period of reconstruction after the Second World War, Marks & Spencer concentrated on offering the customer the best quality at the most competitive prices. In order to achieve this end, Marks & Spencer introduced a series of price cuts over the course of the 1950s and 1960s. Along with the company's emphasis on the provision of quality clothing, these price cuts enabled the company to consolidate its influence by increasing its market share of clothing.

In 1954, for example, *St Michael News* announced: 'M&S Nylons Break the Price Barrier – Quality Maintained at 4*s* 11*d*'.[4] The headline referred to thirty-denier nylon stockings and the company boasted that 'There is no one else in the country selling a stocking of comparable quality at the price' (*St Michael News*, August 1954, No. 9, 'Nylon Special': 1). Marks & Spencer added that 'We are maintaining the identical quality despite the price reduction, and are even working for further improvements' (ibid.). Over the course of the first half of the 1950s, Marks & Spencer doubled its market share in nylons from 5 to 10 per cent, and was selling fifteen million pairs of stockings by 1954. In 1955, the average price of a pair of St Michael stockings had been reduced by about 25 per cent, and at the same time, the cheaper pair of stockings was, according to Marks & Spencer, a vastly improved product. A series of further price cuts followed in 1955 and 1956, as part of a wider campaign on the part of the company to 'reduce prices and combat the challenge of increased living costs', not only in nylons, but also in other clothing ranges, for example footwear and men's trousers (*St Michael News*, 31 March 1956: 1).

Marks & Spencer promoted these lower-price campaigns with its own in-store advertising, using red 'New Lower Price' tickets with the words 'Quality Maintained' written underneath. Significantly, the campaigns received coverage in the local and national press. *St Michael News* reported that even in New York, *Women's Wear Daily* had announced that the 'largest UK chain drops nylon prices, by six to fourteen cents a pair' (*St Michael News*, 2 June 1956: 1). Alongside the lower prices, the company concentrated on 'good housekeeping' (better administration of the business both in stores and at head office), so that savings could be passed on to the customer. In April 1958, the company reported that since these campaigns had begun, Marks & Spencer had reduced the prices of over forty-one million garments sold annually by the company (*St Michael News*, April 1958: 1) (Fig. 30).

But this was only the beginning. In the late 1950s, there were further price cuts, culminating in 1962 with the biggest reductions to date. Not only did the development of synthetic fabrics make clothing easy-care and hard-wearing, but it also reaped benefits in terms of offering customers reduced prices. For example, the price of Marks & Spencer Terylene/worsted permanently pleated skirts was reduced, while prices of nylons, knitwear (including fully fashioned Orlon sweaters), pyjamas and men's Terylene/cotton shirts also came down. By 1967, the reductions made by Marks & Spencer on many ranges of goods brought prices down to make them as much as 12.5 per cent lower than they had been only a year earlier (*St Michael News*, April 1967: 3). The price reductions not only benefited the customer but the company too, Marks & Spencer reporting even as early as 1958 that turnover and profits had increased (*St Michael News*, June 1958: 1).

By the late 1960s, a majority of the major chains were also announcing price cuts. The *Financial Times* reported in 1967 how throughout the high street, retailers were competing for customers especially in nylon goods: while Marks & Spencer and Woolworth led the competition for men's nylon shirts, other stores such as BHS, some Co-ops, Dorothy Perkins and Etam, for example, had also been reducing their prices since 1966 (*Financial Times*, 28 February 1967). Having been more expensive than Marks & Spencer in the 1920s, significantly C&A had become cheaper than its rival (for some items at least), having announced price cuts as early as 1951 (unpublished papers, C&A Archive, HAT). For example, while Marks & Spencer sold 'permanently pleated, crease-resisting, washable Terylene skirts with pure wool at 57*s* 6*d* in 1957[5] (Fig. 1), C&A was selling what would appear to be similar items for less: 49*s* 11*d* in 1959[6] (unpublished papers, C&A Archive, HAT). Overall, these price cuts were partly attributable to cuts in the prices of raw materials. For example, both Du Pont (for Orlon) and Courtaulds (for Courtelle) had been able to reduce the

St Michael NEWS

MARKS & SPENCER LTD.
VOL 6 No 2 FEBRUARY 1959

Only Marks & Spencer could have taken this picture

EVERY ITEM of St. Michael merchandise on this picture — and many more — will have a new lower price from February 5. It is a picture which only Marks and Spencer could have taken, and it is part of an overall scheme which is going to save St. Michael customers over two million pounds.

These latest price reductions, which open the 1959 New Lower Price campaign, represent the company's largest promotional effort so far.

On the morning of Thursday, February 5, millions of people all over the British Isles will pick up their daily paper to see an announcement, worth in its effect, many pounds to them.

In the evening thousands of Londoners hurrying home from work will have the message repeated in their *Star, News* and *Standard*.

A visit to any of the company's 237 stores will show that there are new prices for anything from shirts to socks, jersey dresses to fisherman's knit sweaters, nylons to pyjamas, children's coats to bedjackets.

You can read the full New Lower Price List on page 4. In scope and magnitude it represents a contribution in the war against rising prices which is unique in the history of retailing.

It has been made possible by a combination of things: falls in the prices of some raw materials — and wool in particular, the closest and most imaginative co-operation of our suppliers, and the better administration of the business in store and office. Of these the last — and the efforts made at all levels which it represents — is by no means the least important.

30: 'Only Marks & Spencer Could Have Taken this Picture', *St Michael News*, February 1959.

prices of their acrylics by up to 20 per cent. At Marks & Spencer, reductions in Shetland and lambswool knitwear also reflected the decrease in world prices of raw materials, although Marks & Spencer attributed them mostly to the increased productivity and efficiency of their suppliers.

Overall, in the ten-year period from 1956 to 1966, Israel Sieff recalls that Marks & Spencer more than doubled its share of the British clothing market. At the end of this period, the company's textile sales accounted for about 10 per cent of the national total spent on clothing, and profits after tax more than trebled (I. Sieff 1970: 183–4). In some sectors of the business, however, the share of the market dominated by Marks & Spencer was greater than one-third. By the early 1960s, claimed Israel's son, Marcus, Marks & Spencer had 'changed from being a successful chain of stores into a national institution … By the time Lord Marks died in 1964, there were thousands of families in which the wife and children were largely clothed by Marks & Spencer' (M. Sieff 1988: 232).

FASHION FOR THE PEOPLE

An article promoting slippers 'for all the family', which appeared in *St Michael News* in 1953, is of particular interest because it describes how the company perceived its typical customer, exemplified by the fictitious Barleycorn family, who 'live in a quiet, unpretentious house in a north London suburb'. The article continues:

> They are very happy, moderately prosperous and are typical of a large slice of British working people. They have a radio, would like to be able to afford a TV, do the pools every week, and worry about the same things as thousands of other families do. (*St Michael News*, August 1953, 'Slipper Special': 3)

What repeatedly comes across in the pages of *St Michael News* in the 1950s is the way Marks & Spencer aspired to clothe the whole family. For example, 'fisherman's knit' jumpers, originally a 'fashion novelty' for women, became 'an important part of the knitwear story for all the family' (*St Michael News*, 18 March 1955: 3). Although Marks & Spencer had initially targeted women – this was where the gap in the market really had been in the 1920s and 1930s – from the 1950s, menswear ranges such as shirts, trousers, knitwear, ties and underwear formed an integral part of the Marks & Spencer offer.

Not only did the company aim to cater for whole families, but by the 1970s, argues Briggs (and I would argue perhaps as early as the late 1950s), Marks & Spencer was 'increasingly servicing the whole social spectrum' (Briggs 1984: 79). According to Edward Sieff (chairman 1967–72), one garment in every eight sold in Britain at this time 'carries our famous [St Michael] label' (*St Michael News*, April 1972: 8). Marks & Spencer's explanation for its success was the quality and value of its merchandise, as the following extract from *St Michael News* illustrates:

> To the vast public of thirteen million we serve each week, the name, Marks &
> Spencer, means far more than a nationwide chain of retail stores. These words –
> and the affectionate nickname, Marks and Sparks – have come to be synonyms
> for *quality* and *value*. (ibid.)

Some forty years previously, Simon Marks had told the shareholders at the annual general meeting: 'We are paying increasing attention to the quality and finish of our goods … We see no reason why an article, because it is low-priced, should not have most of the refinements and neatness of a higher-priced article' (Chairman's Annual Statements, 1931, Marks & Spencer Archive). Simon Marks's belief in the democracy of dress and the ways in which he executed his philosophy of retailing were to transform the role of the high street in making fashion available to an increasing sector of the market.

When Simon Marks died in 1964, one of the most striking achievements attributed to this extraordinary man in his obituaries is the extent to which he brought the possibility of fashion into the lives of millions of people to whom fashion had previously been the preserve of the rich: 'He brought high fashion within the reach of every typist and shop assistant and filled the streets of Britain with prettily dressed women' (*Daily Express*, 9 December 1964). In *The Guardian*, he was described as having been 'responsible for a democratic revolution in dress for the British woman' (*The Guardian*, 9 December 1964).

The levelling of the social hierarchy may be seen as both cause and effect of the developments in clothing retailing at Marks & Spencer. This study provides a good example of how the production of fashion cannot be studied in isolation from its consumption, and vice versa. It also suggests ways in which clothing is a pervasive cultural force in society and the manner in which it is retailed provides one of the most visible clues to wider social changes as they occurred in the twentieth century, and especially from the 1920s onwards. Hence the importance of the study of dress in the context of social history needs to be reiterated. Furthermore, when assessing the contribution made by Marks & Spencer to fashion in the twentieth century, this study has highlighted the importance of adopting a historical perspective. To focus on, for example, the positive (early 1990s) or the negative (late 1990s) media 'hype' of the last decade of the twentieth century tends to skew a longer, evolutionary perspective in which the employment, say, of design consultants or supermodels by the company is viewed as a development of, rather than a radical departure from, previous company policy.

This study has attempted to assess the long-term contribution made by Marks & Spencer to redefining fashion: the company's role in removing the stigma attached to ready-made clothing and thus making it acceptable – *desirable* even – to buy clothes from a high-street multiple. Over the course of the twentieth century, fashionable, quality clothing became available to a vastly extended customer range in terms of social background and economic status. While retailers such as Burton's concentrated on achieving this objective for men, Marks & Spencer focused initially on womenswear, extending their offer to children and men soon afterwards, so that by the 1950s they targeted entire families. The company was least successful when it came to offering desirable clothing to teenagers and could not compete with the boutiques catering specifically for this market in the 1960s and 1970s. While over the course of the second half of the twentieth century, Marks & Spencer steadily increased its market share both in the UK and abroad, at the same time, what is termed 'fashion' has altered, perhaps imperceptibly. The terms 'fashion' and 'clothing' have become more easily interchangeable (except perhaps for a minority of fashion aficionados) than they ever were in the past: the upshot of the mass production and mass retailing of clothing was that fashion came to mean good-quality, well-designed, comfortable, technologically innovative (in terms of new fabrics), hard-wearing and easy-care clothing which is available to all, as distinct from higher-priced clothing available only to a few. In short, fashion considered both as a popular term and as a tool for analysis has been democratized.

I pointed out at the beginning that this book would not attempt to offer an explanation of the difficulties faced by Marks & Spencer from the point at which the company's profits took a nosedive in the autumn of 1998, other than in so far as the latter might make reference to changes in, and the evolution of, the consumer market in general. Not surprisingly, much has been made of Marks & Spencer's fortunes at the close of the twentieth century and beginning of the twenty-first. Interestingly, Alex Brummer posited that 'When M&S hurts, so do we. It is not just a barometer of the retail sector, the stock market and the national economy, it is part of our psyche' (*The Guardian*, 5 November 1998: 2). This was an extremely volatile period for the high street as a whole and also one in which C&A closed its doors to customers in Britain, while Littlewoods closed its doors one-and-all. (Marks & Spencer, having bought nineteen stores from Littlewoods, then faced the challenge of integrating these with its existing outlets.)

Ironically, the past strengths of the company's approach to the retailing of clothing – the emphasis on quality and value; the importance of selling clothing not only to whole families (as exemplified by the Barleycorn family referred to above), but to the whole social spectrum, appeared to be either weaknesses or increasingly untenable in the context of the niche marketing of the late twentieth century. The verdict of an article in *The Sunday Times* was unequivocal: 'Marks has lost its reputation for value and quality' (Rushe and Hamilton, *The Sunday Times*, 19 December 1999: 5). On the one hand, Marks & Spencer clothing could not compete in terms of price in a market where supermarkets such as Asda and Tesco, or chains such as Matalan and Primark, were selling much cheaper clothing successfully. Indeed, Marks & Spencer's clothing offer seemed expensive. 'The logic', observed fashion writer Lisa Armstrong, 'of pile it high and sell it not so cheap was the antithesis of the original ethos of providing quality for the masses' (*The Times*, 26 November 1999: 43). On the other hand, quality itself was becoming defined more overtly by style and design (and designer labels) than by what Marks & Spencer had come to represent. The high-fashion pieces sold by Marks & Spencer in the mid-1990s and eulogized in the press were no longer being sold by the late 1990s (and may, in any case, have been too fashionable for a majority of Marks & Spencer customers). At the same time, points out Grace Bradberry, 'a new mood of bohemianism has swept through the British scene and the emphasis is on stunningly impractical pieces – Dolce & Gabbana's leopard-print chiffon coat, Clements Ribeiro's loud flowery dresses' (Bradberry, *The Times*, 19

May 1997: 17). Meanwhile, Marks & Spencer kept silent about the numerous designer associations it had forged (Chapter 4) and clung to the St Michael label. In response to the question posed about what had gone wrong, Susannah Barron wrote, 'M&S might have been the first high-street giant to secure designer input, but other big names are now doing the same, and they, unlike modest old M&S, are screaming it from the rooftops (Barron, *The Guardian*, 5 November 1998: 2). The eventual abandonment of the St Michael brand and the openness with which the company began to promote its associations with designers at the start of the twenty-first century reveal that Marks & Spencer policies had shifted under the pressure of changing market conditions.

Let those who dare predict the future…

INTRODUCTION

1. Harry Sacher, unpublished history, Marks & Spencer Archive, Chapter V: 30. Harry Sacher was Simon Marks's brother-in-law (he was married to Simon's younger sister, Miriam). Although Sacher gives no precise date for when he wrote this history, it is clear from Chapter VI that it was at some point before the demise of the Utility clothing scheme, probably therefore in the late 1940s. Goronwy Rees (1973 [1969]) draws widely on Sacher's work.

2. In its original form, 'trickle-down' theory is generally attributed to G. Simmel (1904) and was made explicit in an article, 'Fashion', originally published in *The International Quarterly*. The theory provides a dynamic for the diffusion of tastes and styles throughout society, based on the presumed propensity to emulate, expressed as a drive towards upward social mobility. Simmel explains: 'Just as soon as the lower classes begin to copy their [the upper classes'] style, thereby crossing the line of demarcation the upper classes have drawn … the upper classes turn away from this style and adopt a new one, which in its turn differentiates them from the masses; and thus the game goes merrily on' (1904: 135). One of the criticisms of Simmel's theory, as originally formulated, was that it had no historical specificity. Furthermore, the theory offers an explanation for luxury goods but reinforces the neglect of the way in which non-luxury clothing contributes to the widening of the market (Fine and Leopold 1993: 140). For example, the mass production and marketing of men's clothing derives less, point out Fine and Leopold, from the tradition of bespoke tailoring than from the early ready-to-wear markets for cheap work clothes for those without direct access to tailoring services, such as sailors, domestic servants and so on: 'It was price and utility that sold these basic garments, not fashion. Styles were often limited and style changes infrequent, allowing manufacturers to plan production well in advance in sufficient quantities to cover store orders and expected re-orders' (ibid.: 232). A much more detailed discussion of trickle-down theories is found in Fine and Leopold 1993: 138–47.

3. The same could be said of work published from the 1970s on subcultures. See, for example, Hebdige (1979) and (1988); and McRobbie (1989) and (1991).

4. Histories of individual companies, such as Eric Sigsworth's *Montague Burton: The Tailor of Taste* (1990) are written from a largely empirical, business-history perspective and do not intend to assess the contribution of the menswear manufacturing and retailing giant in a context of the history of dress. More general histories of shopping itself, such as Alison Adburgham's *Shops and Shopping 1800–1914* (1981), provide useful insights into the history of shopping as it existed for middle- and upper-class women, but for a project with such a large scope, there can only be cursory discussions of the products themselves. Adburgham's *Liberty: Biography of a Shop* (1975), on the other hand, has a strong focus on the products (including clothing) sold, but like Michael Miller's *The*

Bon Marché: Bourgeois Culture and the Department Store (1981) it focuses on middle-class culture and the middle-class shopping experience. As Miller explains, the Bon Marché was 'essentially a middle-class institution' and before the First World War, the chief beneficiaries were the bourgeoisie more so than the working classes (Miller 1981: 165).

5. See, for example, Rees (1973) and Briggs (1984). Former Marks & Spencer archivist Paul Bookbinder researched the Second World War period in *Marks and Spencer: The War Years 1939–1945* (1989). Otherwise, general histories of Marks & Spencer are written by family members from an autobiographical standpoint: see I. Sieff (1970), and M. Sieff (1988 [1986]). Marcus Sieff discusses the Marks & Spencer philosophy of business management in *On Management: The Marks and Spencer Way* (1990). More recently, Bevan (2002 [2001]) discusses why the company's fortunes took a downturn in the late 1990s, focusing, for example, on the 'succession' issue of who would take up Sir Richard Greenbury's role as chief executive. Both Bevan's work and more general analytical research on the clothing industry as a whole such as Jones (2002) are targeted towards a consideration of current and future issues in the retailing and clothing industries.

6. Fine and Leopold, for example, see its shortcomings in the context of it being based on the trickle-down theory (through the supposed emulation by domestic servants of upper-class styles), in which the tastes of the latter are paramount while the income and consumption habits of the labouring classes are ignored (Fine and Leopold 1993: 120; 136). Meanwhile, dress historian Lou Taylor points out, for example, that McKendrick does not study the garments themselves (Taylor 2002: 13).

7. The work of Beverley Lemire (1991; 1997) unusually considers both the production and consumption aspects of the textile and clothing industries. Chapman (1993), on the other hand, tends to focus on the production side of the ready-made clothing industry. Pamela Sharpe (1995), however, does consider the retailing aspect of the ready-made clothing industry in the London area in the mid-nineteenth century.

1. Marks & Spencer, Retailing and the Ready-to-wear Clothing Industry

1. There appears to be some dispute as to the date of Michael Marks' birth. Goronwy Rees dates it as 1863 (Rees 1973: 2). Asa Briggs, however, writes, 'There is no birth certificate for Michael Marks, although it is said that his mother died in giving birth at Slonim in the Russian Polish province of Grodno in June 1859. That is the date given in his naturalization papers in 1897...' (Briggs 1984: 17).

2. The term 'retail revolutionary' is attributed to Simon Marks in the title of Paul Bookbinder's (former Marks & Spencer archivist) biography (Bookbinder 1993).

3. First published in 1969, Rees's study reached the best-seller lists. It was revised in 1973 and all page references in this text are from the latter edition. Rees acknowledges Harry Sacher's unpublished history (see Introduction), from which much of Rees's account of the early history of Marks & Spencer seems to have been taken.

4. The sum of £5 in 1884 was equivalent to £318.56 in 2002. Here and in subsequent chapters, in order to give some indication of a comparative cost, where contemporary prices or cash sums are cited, I give the equivalent monetary value for 2002. To do this I have referred to J. J. McCusker

(2003), 'The Purchasing Power of the British Pound 1264–2002', Economic History Services, <http://www.eh.net/hmit/ppowerbp/>.

5. The sum of £20 in 1884 was equivalent to £1,274.23 in 2002.

6. The transition from open to covered markets was the pattern over much of the north of England. For example, a covered municipal market hall had been built in Liverpool as early as 1822 – a spacious building lit by gas and supplied with fresh water. Liverpool was exceptional, however, and municipal control of markets did not become general until the very end of the century, by which time most of the market trade had already moved into fixed shops (Davis 1966: 254).

7. The sum of 15s in 1890 was equivalent to £50.46 in 2002.

8. This trend continued with, for example, the introduction of the company's staff welfare system in the 1930s, pioneered by Flora Solomon.

9. The sum of 1d in 1884 was equivalent to 27p in 2002.

10. Self-selection was not entirely new, and had been practised by, for example, the Bazaar in Manchester (established 1831), later to become the famous department store of Kendal, Milne & Faulkner in 1836. Here, prices were marked on all the goods and the main advantage was that the customer could walk round and look at everything without feeling any obligation to buy (Adburgham 1981: 138).

11. The sum of £30,000 in 1903 was equivalent to £1,969,766.33 in 2002.

12. London and the large provincial towns – especially Birmingham and Manchester – were well known for their street markets selling all kinds of second-hand clothing. Men's clothing was the most highly valued, in particular frock coats, which would sell (c. 1850) for anything between 2s 6d (equivalent to £8.78 in 2002) and 5s (equivalent to £17.56 in 2002), whereas the cheapest ready-made frock coat sold by H. D. Nicholl of Regent Street was 18s (equivalent to £63.23 in 2002) (Ginsburg 1980: 127). Taking price into account, and considering that the second-hand version was likely to be superior in quality, it is not surprising that the latter was usually more desirable than a new one.

13. The sum of 6d in 1910 was equivalent to £1.56 in 2002.

14. The sum of 5s in 1928 was equivalent to £9.21 in 2002. The five-shilling limit remained in operation until 1939 (the 2002 equivalent being £9.47).

15. The sum of 3d in 1909 was equivalent to 80p in 2002; 6d in 1909 was equivalent to £1.59 in 2002.

16. According to the 1861 census, just under 7 per cent of all workers in England and Wales were engaged in the manufacture of clothing (Fraser 1981: 175).

17. The sum of 12s 6d in 1908 was equivalent to £39.90 in 2002.

18. The sum of £10,000 in 1850 was equivalent to £702,501.37 in 2002.

19. By the 1870s and 1880s, machinery was being applied to other manufacturing processes, for example, felling (stitching down seams) and collar padding. For pressing, however, hand irons – heated by coals and later by gas – were used. In 1905, Don Hoffman, a New York tailor, invented a steam press but it was not widely used until the First World War, when its advantages for the production of uniforms were recognized.

20. The sum of 11s 9d in 1906 was equivalent to £38.62 in 2002.

21. The sum of 1s 9d in 1906 was equivalent to £5.75 in 2002.

22. For example, in 1872 Thomas Lipton started a one-man grocery shop in Glasgow. Within eighteen years, he had seventy branches in London and only eight years after this, 254 branches scattered all over the UK. This rapid growth slowed down after 1918, however, by which time the company had attained its optimum number of stores (see Davis 1966: 283).

23. As Wilson and Taylor point out, the Co-operative Societies' dividend schemes also enabled holders to save for clothes for the family.

2. The Role of Technological Innovation

1. Quoted in obituary for Israel Sieff in *The Times*, 15 February 1972.

2. Sieff, D., 'The Changing Role of Technology', 20 October 1981. This is the text of a presentation given to the board, Marks & Spencer Archive.

3. The following information is derived from unpublished papers, Marks & Spencer Archive.

4. An earlier article reported that Claremont's 'drop in profits for 1995 [was] due to continuing pressure on margins and unexpectedly high contributions to end-of-season markdowns'. Pressures on Marks & Spencer not to increase their prices inevitably affected suppliers who needed to keep labour costs low and to maintain margins (*Draper's Record*, 23 March 1996: 3).

5. Interview with Michael Terry, design director for the Dewhirst Group, 8 April 1997.

6. See Anon., 'Wear Trial Clothing Procedures of the Clothing Division', 1 August 1991, Marks & Spencer Archive.

7. Glasman, I., 'The Changing Role of Technology', 20 October 1981 (Marks & Spencer Archive). Ismar Glasman joined the textile laboratory in 1950 and later went on to become director of technology. By 1966, he was head of the colour department. His particular achievements (up to 1970) were the 'advancement of colour standardization, fastness properties and the improvement of not only yarn and fabrics, but also of items such as buttons and sewing threads used in garment-making' (*St Michael News*, June 1970: 6). He received a gold medal from the Society of Dyers and Colourists for 'exceptional contributions to the improvement in quality of finished textiles in retail outlets' (*St Michael News*, March 1982: 2), retiring from Marks & Spencer in 1982 after thirty-two years with the company. I am very grateful to Mr Glasman for allowing me to interview him (20 January 1997) and for providing me with invaluable information for this chapter.

8. I am grateful to Fred Redding, company archivist for Selfridges in the 1990s, who supplied me with information regarding Selfridges' textile laboratory, thus highlighting the unique function of Marks & Spencer's textile laboratory in the 1930s. See also Jopp (1965: 52), who points out that in 1946, a quality control department was established at the St Margaret Works of the Marks & Spencer supplier Corah. Corah also had a textile laboratory well before Marks & Spencer made it a requirement for suppliers to carry out their own tests on the merchandise they manufactured (Interview with Ismar Glasman, 20 January 1997).

9. This information is taken from Christopher Salmon, 'Scientific Method and Technical Services in Marks & Spencer', March 1957: 4 (Marks & Spencer Archive).

10. The sum of £1 in 1932 was equivalent to £42.44 in 2002.

11. Salmon points out: 'When, in 1940–41, the Board of Trade adopted the Utility scheme, it actually took over as Utility fabrics many of the cloth standards that had been evolved by the merchandise

development department' (March 1957: 6, Marks & Spencer Archive). See also Bookbinder 1993: 124.

12. *Textile Bulletin* No. 1, 27 February 1945, Marks & Spencer Archive. In subsequent bulletins, developments in different kinds of rayon and in cotton, wool and nylon are discussed, as well as advances in fabric/fibre production processes, including dyeing (see also *Textile Bulletin* Nos. 2–12).

13. Interview with Ismar Glasman, 20 January 1997. Lewis Goodman (who joined Marks & Spencer in about 1947) was closely involved with the introduction of easy-care synthetic fabrics. Moving to the merchandise development department, Mr Goodman later became an executive when textile technology was set up in 1965 and director of textile technology when he joined the board in 1968.

14. This was certainly the view expressed at a meeting I attended in the women's suits department, where 70 per cent of the fabric for the autumn 1996 range was new (Suppliers' Briefing, 28 March 1996). I am grateful to Sara Stephenson (Gottgens), former range selector for women's suits, for inviting me to attend this meeting.

15. The principal reason for choosing the Pantheon store in Oxford Street was because of its status as one of the 'top stores', given priority for receiving new lines of merchandise.

16. Correspondence from D. L. Shaw to R. Greenbury, 9 April 1979, Marks & Spencer Archive.

17. The following section is largely based upon the information provided by Ismar Glasman in an interview (20 January 1997).

18. A further step in the establishment of the standardization of lighting took place in 1976 when Marks & Spencer announced the introduction of a new system of fluorescent lighting which was to be common to all stores, and incorporated into all light boxes, known as Philips TL84. The system represented a major breakthrough because it combined good colour rendering with very high luminous efficiency and also provided a 30–40 per cent saving in electricity charges when it was first introduced in the 1970s (*St Michael News*, March 1976: 3).

3. Marks & Spencer and Fashion: The Importance of Design

1. According to Eric Estorick's unpublished *History of Marks & Spencer* (Marks & Spencer Archive), the design department was established in 1938 (Chapter XIII: 2). Israel Sieff and his son Marcus Sieff also cite this date (I. Sieff 1970: 181 and M. Sieff 1988: 233).

2. Interview with Ismar Glasman, 20 January 1997. See Chapter 2 for more information on Glasman's role at Marks & Spencer.

3. This information is taken from a booklet (Marks & Spencer Archive) drawn from a series of articles appearing in the May, June and July 1953 issues of *Fashions and Fabrics*. According to a 'development report' for 1950, Hans Schneider refers to the new pattern-cutting and grading section as 'the most important development in the designing department during the month of December ... With this section as a 'liaison', we hope to create a unique service for our manufacturers, who should receive the new styles together with faultlessly graded patterns' (5).

4. I am grateful to Richard Lachlan for the useful information he provided to me in an interview (10 May 1996). Mr Lachlan trained at the Royal College of Art and worked with designer Victor Stiebel before joining Marks & Spencer as a designer from 1968 to 1988.

5. I am grateful to former Marks & Spencer archivist Susan Breakell for informing me of the existence of these letters and documents.

6. The sum of £3,000 in 1952 was equivalent to £53,020.37 in 2002.

7. The sum of £200 in 1957 was equivalent to £2,960.09 in 2002.

8. The sum of 6s 11d in 1957 was equivalent to £5.12 in 2002.

9. The sum of £21 in 1976 was equivalent to £92.92 in 2002.

10. Caroline Evans, for example, makes reference to the chain-store endorsements of designers such as Hussein Chalayan working for Topshop and Jasper Conran for Debenhams (Breward, Ehrman and Evans 2004: 158).

4. Selling Fashion

1. Subsequently stores were opened in Liverpool (1924); Birmingham (1926); Manchester (1928). The information about C&A was sourced at the National Advertising Trust at Raveningham, Norfolk, which inherited the C&A archive when the company stopped trading in the UK in 2001.

2. The sum of 5s in 1922 was equivalent to £8.34 in 2002.

3. Report by consultants Taylor Nelson, 22 July 1991, Marks & Spencer Archive.

4. The sum of £1 in 1987 was equivalent to £1.73 in 2002.

5. These figures were given courtesy of *The M&S Magazine*, Redwood Publishing.

6. The sum of £50,000 in 1981 was equivalent to £117,797.53 in 2002.

7. In 1963, Marks & Spencer 'advertised' the biggest-ever fashion show to date. It was in aid of the NSPCC and was held at Manchester's Free Trade Hall to a total audience of over 2,500 (see *St Michael News*, January 1963: 1).

8. The sum of £180,000 raised from ticket sales was donated to charity (*Draper's Record*, 7 October 1995: 4).

9. Attributed to Lord (Israel) Sieff and cited in Rees (1973: 250).

10. By the end of 1986, Lord Rayner (chairman, 1984–1991) announced in his Christmas message to staff that, to date, 46,451 sq. metres (500,000 sq. ft) of selling space had been added, as had twenty-five extensions, and half of Marks & Spencer's total floor space had been modernized (*St Michael News*, December 1986: 1).

11. In 1954, Burton's transferred their account to W. S. Crawford, the ninth largest advertising business in Britain, and this coincided with a heavy burst of advertising in the national press (Mort 1996: 142).

12. For Burton's, Mort describes the 1950s as a period of reassessment for the role of the window display. There was now a need for the display to show a theme, not just to display a huge range of merchandise, and by 1964, Burton's display department had a staff of over 400, who were kept up to date via a central advisory bureau in Leeds (Mort 1996: 140).

13. In 1999, Marks & Spencer's online shopping offered an initial range of 200 products 'with the ambition', observes Godbold, 'of reaching 3,000, of which approximately one-third was anticipated to be clothing within two years of operation. This would represent the equivalent of a 5,600 square-metre [60,277 sq. ft] store, in other words, a range of products only represented in the largest ten of the group's outlets' (Godbold 2000: 112–3).

5. Marks & Spencer and the Internationalization of Fashion

1. I am grateful to Alan Lambert, former Marks & Spencer divisional director for European merchandise, for agreeing to be interviewed (18 December 1995) and for his help in accessing useful information for this chapter.

2. This figure covered all Marks & Spencer merchandise except for food and certain textiles such as chiffon scarves – see *St Michael News*, 25 February 1955: 1 and June 1959: 4.

3. In the context of this discussion it is worth noting that in the early 1980s, according to Marks & Spencer, approximately 25 per cent of all clothing production in the UK was for Marks & Spencer and it was calculated that 170,000 people were employed making, distributing and selling St Michael goods (*St Michael News*, November 1982: 1).

4. In Canada, however, this trend was reversed towards the end of the 1980s, with the decision made to sell more British-made clothing – see report in *St Michael News*, May/June 1990: 1.

5. This figure does not include the 189 Brooks Brothers stores, 119 in the USA and 70 in Japan, and two Brooks Brothers franchises in Hong Kong (Anon., 1998, *Company Facts*).

6. Anon., 'Marks and Spencer European Development 1976–1988 and the Future', 1988, Marks & Spencer Archive.

7. According to Derek Hayes, director for European operations, European summer ranges could be tested six months earlier in South Africa (quoted in *Draper's Record*, 23 March 1996: 12).

8. At the time, *Draper's Record* reported, the German market was the biggest in Europe with the Cologne store having a catchment area of 17 million people within an hour's drive of it. This development was especially significant therefore in Marks & Spencer's campaign to conquer the European market (*Drapers Record, DR Focus*, 7 September 1996: viii).

Conclusion

1. Briggs argues, for example, that the opening of the Pantheon store at 178 Oxford Street in October 1938 'introduced into M&S retailing the full flavour of the upper income bracket department store' (Briggs 1984: 47). The designer of the new store was Robert Lutyens, son of the famous architect, Sir Edwin Lutyens.

2. Quoted in *St Michael News*, August 1965: 7. Clearly, the fact that Marks & Spencer referred to this article is illustrative of the 'classless' image the company wanted to create for itself.

3. Quoted in Wilson and Taylor (1989: 93), and taken from de la Haye, unpublished MA thesis, Royal College of Art, 1986, 'The Role of Design within the Commercialization of Women's Ready-to-wear Clothing in Britain during the Inter-war Years, with Specific Reference to the Cheapest Levels of Production'.

4. The sum of 4*s* 11*d* in 1954 was equivalent to £4.14 in 2002.

5. The sum of 57*s* 6*d* in 1957 was equivalent to £42.55 in 2002.

6. The sum of 49*s* 11*d* in 1959 was equivalent to £35.66 in 2002.

BIBLIOGRAPHY

Adburgham, A. (1975), *Liberty: Biography of a Shop*, London: George Allen and Unwin.

—— (1981 [1964]), *Shops and Shopping 1800–1914*, London: Barrie and Jenkins.

Beazley, A. (1973), 'The Heavy and Light Clothing Industries 1850–1920', *Costume*, 7: 55–9.

Bennett, A. (1990 [1908]), *The Old Wives' Tale*, Harmondsworth: Penguin.

Bevan, J. (2002 [2001]), *The Rise and Fall of Marks & Spencer*, London: Profile Books.

Bookbinder, P. (1989), *Marks & Spencer: The War Years 1939–1945*, London: Century Benham.

—— (1993), *Simon Marks: Retail Revolutionary*, London: Weidenfeld and Nicolson.

Bowles, G. and Kirrane, S. (1990), *Knitting Together: Memories of Leicestershire's Hosiery Industry*, Leicester: Leicestershire Museums, Arts and Record Service.

Breward, C. (1995), *The Culture of Fashion: A New History of Fashionable Dress*, Manchester and New York: Manchester University Press.

—— (2003), *Fashion*, Oxford: Oxford University Press.

—— (2004), *Fashioning London: Clothing and the Modern Metropolis*, Oxford and New York: Berg.

—— Ehrman, E. and Evans, C. (2004), *The London Look: Fashion from Street to Catwalk*, New Haven and London: Yale University Press and the Museum of London.

Brewer, J. and Porter, R. (eds.) (1993), *Consumption and the World of Goods*, London and New York: Routledge.

Briggs, A. (1956), *Friends of the People: The Centenary History of Lewis's*, London: Batsford.

—— (1984), *Marks and Spencer 1884–1994: A Centenary History*, London: Octopus Books.

Burns, W. (1959), *British Shopping Centres: New Trends in Layout and Distribution*, London: Leonard Hill Books.

Chapman, S. (1993), 'The Innovating Entrepreneurs in the British Ready-Made Clothing Industry', *Textile History*, 24 (1): 5–25.

Charles-Roux, E. (1982), *Chanel And Her World*, London: Weidenfeld and Nicolson.

—— (1989), *Chanel*, London: Collins Harvill.

Craik, J. (1993), *The Face of Fashion: Cultural Studies in Fashion*, London and New York: Routledge.

Davis, D. (1966), *A History of Shopping*, London: Routledge and Kegan Paul.

De la Haye, A. (1986), 'The Role of Design within the Commercialization of Women's Ready-to-wear Clothing in Britain during the Inter-war Years, with Specific Reference to the Cheapest Levels of Production', unpublished MA thesis, Royal College of Art.

—— (ed.) (1996), *The Cutting Edge: 50 Years of British Fashion*, London: V&A Publications.

—— and Wilson, E. (eds.) (1999), *Defining Dress: Dress as Object, Meaning and Identity*, Manchester and New York: Manchester University Press.

Ewing, E. (1993 [1974]), *History of 20th Century Fashion*, London: Batsford.

Fine, B. and Leopold, E. (1993), *The World of Consumption*, London and New York: Routledge.

Fraser, H. (1981), *The Coming of the Mass Market 1850–1914*, London: Macmillan.

Ginsburg, M. (1980), 'Rags to Riches: The Second-hand Clothes Trade 1700–1978', *Costume*, 14: 121–35.

Godbold, B. (2000), 'The Chain Store Challenge' in White, N. and Griffiths, I. (eds.) *The Fashion Business: Theory, Practice, Image*, Oxford: Berg.

Gross, M. (1995*), Model: The Ugly Business of Beautiful Women*, London: Bantam Press.

Guy, C. (1994), *The Retail Development Process: Location, Property and Planning*, London and New York: Routledge.

Handley, S. (1999), *Nylon: The Manmade Fashion Revolution*, London: Bloomsbury Publishing.

Hebdige, D. (1979), *Subculture: The Meaning of Style*, London: Methuen.

—— (1988), *Hiding in the Light: On Images and Things*, London: Routledge.

Honeyman, K. (2000), *Well Suited: A History of the Leeds Clothing Industry 1850–1990*, Oxford: Oxford University Press.

Jeffreys, J. B. (1954), *Retail Trading in Britain 1850–1950*, Cambridge: Cambridge University Press.

Jobling, P. (2005), *Man Appeal: Advertising, Modernism and Menswear*, Oxford: Berg.

John, A (ed.) (1985), *Unequal Opportunities: Women's Employment in England 1800–1918*, Oxford: Basil Blackwell.

Jones, R. (2002), *The Apparel Industry*, Oxford: Blackwell Science.

Jopp, K. (1965), *Corah of Leicester 1815–1965*, Leicester: Newman Neame Ltd.

Kawamura, Y. (2005), *Fashion-ology: An Introduction to Fashion Studies*, Oxford: Berg.

Kidwell, C. and Christman, M. (1974), *Suiting Everyone: The Democratization of Clothing in America*, Washington, DC: Smithsonian Institute Press, published for the National Museum of History and Technology.

Lebhar, G. M. (1952), *Chain Stores in America 1859–1950*, New York: Chain Store Publishing Corporation.

Lemire, B. (1991), *Fashion's Favourite: The Cotton Trade and the Consumer in Britain, 1660–1800*, Oxford: Pasold Research Fund/Oxford University Press.

—— (1997), *Dress, Culture and Commerce: The English Clothing Trade before the Factory*, Basingstoke: Macmillan.

Leopold, E. (1992), 'The Manufacture of the Fashion System' in Ash, J. and Wilson, E. (eds.), *Chic Thrills: A Fashion Reader*, London: Pandora.

Levitt, S. (1986), *Victorians Unbuttoned: Registered Designs for Clothing, Their Makers and Wearers 1839–1900*, London: George Allen and Unwin.

Mackrell, A. (1992), *Coco Chanel*, London: Batsford.

McCusker, J. J. (2003), 'The Purchasing Power of the British Pound 1264–2002', in *Economic History Services*, <http://www.eh.net/hmit/ppowerbp/>.

McKendrick, N., Brewer, J. and Plumb, J. H. (1982), *The Birth of a Consumer Society: The Commercialization of Eighteenth-Century England*, London: Europa Publications.

McRobbie, A. (ed.) (1989), *Zoot Suits and Second-hand Dresses*, Basingstoke: Macmillan.

—— (1991), *Feminism and Youth Culture*, Basingstoke: Macmillan.

Melling, J. and Barry, J. (1992), *Culture in History: Production, Consumption and Values in Historical Perspective*, Exeter: Exeter University Press.

Miller, M. (1981), *The Bon Marché: Bourgeois Culture and the Department Store*, Princeton and Chichester: Princeton University Press.

Mort, F. (1996), *Cultures of Consumption: Masculinities and Social Space in Late Twentieth-Century Britain*, London and New York: Routledge.

—— (1997), 'Paths to Mass Consumption: Britain and the USA since 1945' in M. Nava, M. et al. (eds.), *Buy This Book: Studies in Advertising and Consumption*, London and New York: Routledge.

Nava, M., Blake, A., MacRury, I. and Richards, B. (eds.) (1997), *Buy This Book: Studies in Advertising and Consumption*, London and New York: Routledge.

Polhemus, T. (1994), *Street Style: From Sidewalk to Catwalk*, London: Thames and Hudson.

Protheroe, K. (2005), 'Quality Stitch by Stitch: Clothing and Associated Publications Held in the Marks & Spencer Company Archive', *Costume*, 39: 100–112.

Rees, G. (1973 [1969]), *A History of Marks and Spencer*, London: Weidenfeld and Nicolson.

Rendall, J. (1990), *Women in an Industrialising Society: England 1750–1880*, Oxford: Basil Blackwell.

Roberts, E. (1995), *Women and Families: An Oral History 1940–1970*, Oxford: Blackwell.

Roche, D. (1994), *The Culture of Clothing: Dress in the Ancien Régime*, Cambridge: Cambridge University Press.

Sharpe, P. (1995), 'Cheapness and Economy: Manufacturing and Retailing Ready-made Clothing in London and Essex 1830–1850', *Textile History*, 26 (2): 203–13.

Sieff, I. (1970), *The Memoirs of Israel Sieff*, London: Weidenfeld and Nicolson.

Sieff, M. (1988 [1986]), *Don't Ask the Price: The Memoirs of the President of Marks & Spencer*, London: Fontana.

—— (1990), *On Management: The Marks & Spencer Way*, London: Weidenfeld and Nicolson.

Sigsworth, E. (1990), *Montague Burton: The Tailor of Taste*, Manchester and New York: Manchester University Press.

Simmel, G. (1904), 'Fashion', *International Quarterly*, x (1), October: 130–55.

Spufford, M. (1984), *The Great Reclothing of Rural England: Petty Chapmen and their Wares in the Seventeenth Century*, London: Hambledon Press.

Styles, J. (1998), 'Dress in History: Reflections on a Contested Terrain', *Fashion Theory: The Journal of Dress, Body and Culture*, 2 (4): 383–9.

Taylor, L. (1983), *Mourning Dress: A Costume and Social History*, London: George Allen and Unwin.

—— (2002), *The Study Of Dress History*, Manchester and New York: Manchester University Press.

Thompson, E. P. and Yeo, E. (eds.) (1971), *The Unknown Mayhew: Selections from the Morning Chronicle 1849–50*, Harmondsworth: Penguin.

Wilson, A. (ed.) (1993), *Rethinking Social History: English Society 1570–1920 and its Interpretation*, Manchester: Manchester University Press.

Wilson, E. and Taylor, L., (1989), *Through the Looking Glass: A History of Dress from 1860 to the Present Day*, London: BBC Books.

Worth, R. (1999), 'Fashioning the Clothing Product: Technology and Design at Marks & Spencer', *Textile History*, 30 (3): 234–50.

Wray, M. (1957), *The Women's Outerwear Industry*, London: Gerald Duckworth & Co. Ltd.

Newspaper articles

Anon., (1998), 'The Changing Fabric of Italian Fashion', *The Economist*, 11 April: 65–6.

Armstrong, L. (1999), 'How the Forty Something Woman Brought M&S to its Knees', *The Times*, 26 November: 43 and 45.

Barron, S. (1998), 'What's Gone Wrong? Fashion', *The Guardian*, 5 November: 2.

Blanchard, T. (1994), 'Buy Me: Satin Stripe Trousers', *The Independent*, 18 November.

Bradberry, G. (1996), 'Cashmere Finally Shapes Up', *The Times*, 16 November: 3.

—— (1997), 'How Marks Lost its Sparks', *The Times*, 19 May: 17.

Brampton, S. (1994), 'The Adoration of St Michael', *Guardian Weekend*, 8 October: 40–4 and 56.

Brummer, A. (1998), 'Are You Being Served?', *The Guardian*, 5 Novemeber: 2–3.

Cowe, R. (1995), 'M&S Moves into Germany and China', *The Guardian*, 28 March: 15.

—— (1997), 'M&S Breaks the £1 Billion Barrier', *The Guardian*, 21 May: 19.

Frankel, S. (1996), 'Jolly Good Show', *The Guardian*, 7 August: 9.

—— (1998), 'High Hopes', *Guardian Weekend*, 7 February: 38–43.

Glaister, D. (1992), 'Knickers to the French', *The Guardian*, 15 December: 12–13.

Griggs, B. (1976), 'I Wonder … Could M&S for Once Be Slipping Up?', *Daily Mail*, 13 December: 12.

Hume, M. (1994), 'The Shapeless Decade', *The Independent*, 2 December: 21.

Modlinger, J. (1992), 'Get On Your Marks: St Michael Sets the High Street Pace', *Daily Express*, 20 February: 29.

Oldfield, C. (1996), 'Copy-Cats Face the Acid Test', *The Sunday Times*, 27 October: 13.

Ostler, C. (1995), 'Evangelista Glamour Blitz that Failed M&S', *Mail On Sunday*, 16 April: 37 and 39.

Rushe, D. and Hamilton, K. (1999), 'Bargain Basement', *The Sunday Times*, 19 December: 5.

Smith, L. (1993), 'Marks' Sparks', *Evening Standard Magazine*, 29 October: 14–16.

Spencer, M. (1995), 'The Gospel According to St Michael', *Vogue*, April: 26–30.

Tredre, R. (1990), 'Shaping Up for the Hard Sell On the Soft Suit', *The Independent*, 22 September: 32.

—— (1997), 'Taking the Hauteur out of Couture', *The Observer*, 23 February: 16.

Urry, M. (1988), 'St Michael's Quiet Revolution', *Financial Times*, 21 May.

Whitebloom, S. (1996), 'Marks and Spencer's Woolly Jumpers Going to Meet Their Maker', *The Guardian*, 18 October: 22.

Wilkinson, T. (1993), 'M&S to Lift Capital Outlay to £350 Million', *The Independent*, 4 November: 37.

Magazine articles (no author or title given)

Draper's Record, 23 May 1987.

Draper's Record, 27 May 1995: 8.

Draper's Record, 7 October 1995: 4.

Draper's Record, 25 November 1995: 7.

Draper's Record, 23 March 1996: 12.

Draper's Record, 30 March 1996: 3 and 12.

Draper's Record, 10 August 1996: 5.

Draper's Record (*DR Focus*), 7 September 1996: viii.

Draper's Record, 22 February 1997: 4.

Draper's Record, 1 March 1997: 7.

Draper's Record, 5 April 1997: 12.

Financial Times, 28 February 1967.

GQ Magazine, October/ November 1989.

The Guardian, 8 January 1997 (tabloid): 10.

Just Seventeen, 25 October 1989.

Options, Summer 1989: 55.

Papers and publications sourced from the Marks & Spencer Archive

Ambassador Magazine (1967), 'St Michael Spreads Its Wings: Fashions for Spring and Summer 1967'.

Anon. (1938), Checking Lists for the Isle of Man, February.

Anon. (1945), *Textile Bulletin*, Nos. 1–12. See especially No. 1 (27 February).

Anon. (1952), 'Model Dresses Imported from France under Import Licence', 2 January.

Anon. (1953), booklet drawn from a series of articles appearing in the May, June and July issues of *Fashions and Fabrics*.

Anon. (1954), 'Facts About Fabrics'.

Anon. (1954), 'Expenses and Fees Paid to Anny Blatt', 19 February.

Anon. (1954), 'Models Supplied by Madame Anny Blatt, October 1951 – 16 February 1954', 19 February.

Anon. (1971), 'Analysis of Sales by Fibre', February.

Anon. (1975), Textile Dictionary.

Anon. (1983), Report on Size Ratios, 9 November.

Anon. (1988), 'Marks & Spencer European Development 1976–1988 and the Future'.

Anon. (1991), 'Wear Trial Procedures of the Clothing Division', 1 August.

Anon. (1996), Suppliers' Briefing, 28 March.

Anon. (1998), *Company Facts.*

Anon. (1998), *Annual Report and Financial Statements.*

Chairman's Annual Statements (1931).

Estorick, E. (unpublished), *History of Marks & Spencer.*

Glasman, I. to Marks, S. (1953), unpublished memo, 4 November.

Glasman, I. (1969), 'Why Polyester? The Fibre of the 70s' (paper for the Textile Technology Symposium), November.

Glasman, I. to Williams, B. (1981), unpublished memo, 18 September.

Glasman, I. (1981), 'The Changing Role of Technology' (presentation to the main board of directors), 20 October.

Goode, L. (1965), 'Cotton and Man-made Fibres: A Retailer's View' (paper for the Symposium on Inter-Fibre Competition, in conjunction with the 24th Plenary Meeting of the International Cotton Advisory Committee), May.

Goodman, B. to Midland Bank (1957), unpublished letter, 11 July.

Kann, E. (1962), 'Man-made Fibres and the Consumer' (paper for the Second World Congress of Man-made Fibres), 1 May.

Sacher, H. (1940s?), unpublished history (see Note 1, Introduction).

Salmon, C. (1957), 'Scientific Method and Technical Services in Marks & Spencer', March.

Schneider, H. (1950), 'Development Report'.

—— (1973), memo to Marcus Sieff, 5 November.

Shaw, D. L. to Greenbury, R. (1979), unpublished memo, 9 April.

Sieff, D. (1981), 'The Changing Role of Technology' (presentation to the main board of directors), 20 October.

Sieff, M, to Goodman, B. (1951), unpublished memo ref. Anny Blatt, 17 October.

Taylor Nelson (1991), consultants, untitled report on St Michael trademark, 22 July.

Underwood, R. (1981), 'Sourcing Textiles' in 'The Changing Role of Technology' (presentation to the main board of directors), 20 0ctober.

Marks & Spencer Magazine
Summer 1932: 6 and 15–17.

The M&S Magazine (originally Redwood Publishing)
Spring 1988: 78.
Spring 1989: 63.
Winter 1990: 60–1.
Spring 1994: 83.
Summer 1995: 44–5.

M&S World
Autumn 1989: 20.
Winter 1990–91: 8, 9 and 25.
Autumn/Winter 1993–94: 4.
Winter 1995: 2.

St Michael News
June 1953: 1 and 2 and 3.
July 1953: 1–2.
August 1953, 'Autumn Hats Special': 1–2.
August 1953, 'Slipper Special': 1 and 3.
September 1953: 2.
October 1953: 3–4.
November 1953: 1.
January 1954, 'Spring Hats Special': 2.
April 1954: 1.
July 1954: 2.
August 1954: No. 9, 'Nylon Special': 1.
August 1954, No. 10, 'Jerseywear Special': 1.
3 December 1954: 2 and 4.

17 December 1954: 1–2 and 3.
25 February 1955: 1.
18 March 1955: 3 and 5.
10 June 1955: 1.
1 July 1955: 4.
22 July 1955: 3.
7 October 1955: 2.
28 October 1955: 1 and 2.
16 January 1956: 1.
15 February 1956: 3.
31 March 1956: 1.
2 June 1956: 1.
3 August 1956: 2 and 4.
(From 1957, there was one issue monthly so no date is given.)
February 1957: 1.
April 1957: 3.
June 1957: 1.
September 1957: 1.
March 1958: 1 and 4.
April 1958: 1.
May 1958: 1.
June 1958: 1.
July 1958: 2.
September 1958: 4.
November 1958: 2.
December 1958: 1 and 4.
January 1959: 3.
April 1959: 1.
June 1959: 4.
July 1959: 1.
September 1959: 6.
February 1960: 1.
April 1960: 7.
June 1960: 1.
November 1960: 4.
January 1961: 2.
May 1961: 2.
Autumn 1961: 2.
December 1961: 3.
January 1963: 1.
February 1963: 3.

January/February 1965: 1.

June 1965: 1.

August 1965: 7.

October 1966: 1 and 8.

November 1966: 2.

December 1966: 6.

January 1967: 2.

April 1967: 3.

May 1967: 1.

Autumn 1967: 12.

December 1967: 6.

July/August 1969: 3.

Autumn 1969: 3 and 4.

June 1970: 6.

October 1970: 3.

August 1971: 2 and 6.

February 1972: 5.

April 1972: 1, 5 and 8.

June 1972: 3.

November 1972: 1.

July 1974: 3 and 6.

February 1975: 8.

March 1976: 3.

June 1976: 2.

July 1976: 7.

October 1976: 3.

February 1977: 7.

April 1977: 3.

December 1977: 1.

March 1978: 2.

October 1978: 3.

December 1978: 1.

July 1979: 3.

November 1979: 1.

April 1981: 2 and 7.

October 1981: 3.

March 1982: 2.

May 1982: 1.

June 1982: 2.

November 1982: 1.

June 1983: 5–7.

May 1984: 7.
September 1984: 1 and 7.
November 1984: 10.
February 1985: 3.
May 1985: 1.
June 1985: 6.
August 1985: 4.
September 1985: 5.
March 1986:3.
April 1986: 1 and 5.
December 1986: 1.
January 1987: 9.
May 1987: 3 and 5.
August 1987: 1.
November 1987: 8.
April 1988: 2.
May 1988: 7.
September/October 1988: 5.
July 1989: 1.
Christmas Issue, 1989: 1.
March 1990: 2.
May/June 1990: 1.
Summer 1990, 'International News': 3.
September 1990: 3.
March 1995: 8.

Market share information
Verdict on Clothing Retailers (1996): 20.

Interviews conducted by the author
Alan Lambert, 18 December 1995.
Richard Lachlan, 10 May 1996.
Ismar Glasman, 20 January 1997.
Michael Terry, 8 April 1997.
Lewis Goodman, 26 January 1999.

Obituaries
Obituary for Simon Marks, *Daily Express*, 9 December 1964; *The Guardian*, 9 December 1964.
Obituary for Israel Sieff, *The Times*, 15 February 1972; *Jewish Daily Forward* (New York), 15 February 1972.

Television broadcasts
Clothes Show, 10 December 1995, BBC One.
World in Action, 15 January 1996, ITV.

Other archives

The History of Advertising Trust (HAT), Raveningham, Norfolk, with great foresight took on the C&A Archive when the company closed its UK stores in 2001, offering useful comparative material. Advertisements including those for C&A are cited from *Daily Mail,* 21 August 1922; *Daily Chronicle*, 25 September 1922 and *Evening News*, 4 December 1922.

Selfridges Archive, London.

INDEX

Page numbers in *italics* refer to illustrations